THE LONELY PATH
TO FREEDOM

THE LONELY PATH TO FREEDOM

DEREK THROWER

ROBERT HALE · LONDON

© *Derek Thrower 1980*
First published in Great Britain 1980

ISBN 0 7091 8139 6

Robert Hale Limited
Clerkenwell House
Clerkenwell Green
London EC1R 0HT

Typeset by
Art Photoset Ltd., Beaconsfield, Bucks
and printed and bound in Great Britain by
Weatherby Woolnough, Wellingborough, Northants

CONTENTS

1	Shot Down	9
2	Escape	19
3	On The Run	27
4	Kommando 1547	57
5	The Second Escape	65
6	Stalag Luft 3—Sagan	85
7	Barth	93
8	Heydekrug	109
9	Evacuation	123
10	Stalag Luft 6—Grosse Tychau	133
11	The March	137
12	The Final Escape	145

FOR
Mary, Sean, Simeon and Philippa

1

Shot Down

It was the fifteenth of July 1941, and the time was three o'clock in the morning. I was twenty-one years old, dangling from the harness of a parachute, peering anxiously down into the darkness below.

The Wellington bomber from which I had jumped swung in a long steep arc towards the ground and exploded furiously on impact. Moments later I landed on sandy soil, the parachute subsiding gently and enmeshing me in its white folds. With difficulty I unbuckled the harness, gathered the parachute together and buried it in the sand; then, as my knees buckled under me, I collapsed on the ground, and lay there trembling from head to foot. Tension had caught up with me, and I was content to lie there until my jangled nerves made peace with my body.

A few hours earlier, this had been just another routine bombing raid, the target Bremen. But before we even reached the target, on the run-in, the starboard engine of the Wellington blew up. We released our bombs, and I swung the plane round and set course for home.

It was a long unsuccessful struggle. Hounded by searchlights and flak, harassed by a night-fighter, the plane lost height steadily and with the realization that we were not going to make it, I ordered the crew to abandon aircraft. The second pilot checked that they had gone, formally shook hands with me, and was gone himself. At 1,000 feet altitude over the Dutch coast I baled out.

Alone in a Dutch field I sat up and fumbled in my pockets for my pipe, a constant companion. I lit up, and after a few deep pulls at the pipe, was able to relax and look around me. In the distance, the wreck of the bomber was blazing furiously, flames leaping high into the sky, the quietness of the night broken by the sound of exploding ammunition. The pale early morning light revealed nothing but sand, dotted here and there by stunted trees, not a building in sight. A plane droned overhead, on course for England, and for a few moments I felt sorry for myself.

It was time to get moving. The Germans would be here soon, and would seal off the area. My possessions consisted of pipe and tobacco, watch, and a silk map in the lapel of my jacket. Underneath my battledress and trousers I was wearing pyjamas, more comfortable than the regulation underwear. I had large thick socks and flying boots that I would have traded happily for a pair of old army boots.

The light was strengthening. I stood up, looked for the last time at the burning plane, and trudged away westwards across the sandy desolate countryside.

Two hours later I came to an old dilapidated house, small and isolated. I desperately needed to know where I was, and decided to take the risk of asking there: I could always run away if they were hostile. I knocked loudly, and stood back from the door and waited. A man opened the door, his eyes dulled from sleep; behind him stood a woman and a little girl of eight or nine years. I tried to explain who I was and what I wanted to know, but from their bewildered faces I could see that they believed themselves to be confronted by a madman. In desperation I pulled out the silk map, showed it to them, then pointed around the horizon. It was the little girl who understood, and showed me that I had landed near a place called Staphorst, close to the Zuider Zee. She soon grasped the predicament I was in, and I was invited into the house and given food, while the man, by a mixture of nods and grunts and waving of arms, explained that he would get help, and that I was to wait until he returned. While I waited, the child slipped on a pair of clogs and danced for me, encouraged by her mother.

The man returned, and indicated to me to follow him. I felt apprehensive, but did as he said; I still felt confident that I could escape at the first sign of trouble. Outside it was now broad daylight, as we walked together in silence to a large farm dwelling. I followed him into a room full of people, many of them youngsters. They were excited and curious, and plied me with drink and cigarettes. Time went by and the strange language, the sudden outbursts of laughter as well as the general air of excitement, made me uneasy. There seemed to be nobody in charge, it was as if everybody was waiting, and all the time they stared at me but did nothing.

A burst of laughter was cut short in mid-air. Everybody stopped talking. I turned to the door, to face two uniformed men. The men had guns in their hands, and the guns were pointed at me. A voice shouted at me to come, and a gun beckoned me to the door. I walked out of the silent room into the daylight.

With the guards on either side of me, and a gun at my back, I walked along endless paths and tracks. A feeling of loneliness and uncertainty filled my mind. Did the Germans take prisoners? Was I to be shot? We stopped. The guards spoke to each other for a moment, then one turned to me and in English informed me that they were Dutch police, and had been given orders to find me and hand me over to the Germans. He gave me a cigarette and lit it for me, then went on to say that they had no alternative but to carry out their orders; the Dutch would suffer if I was allowed to escape. I indicated that I understood, and thanked him for their courtesy, and we resumed our march.

This moment of familiarity was quickly over—a column of dust rising behind a line of trees on the horizon agitated my captors; the Germans were on their way. The policemen wished me well and asked me to forgive them once more. The dust became a car which drew up on the road ahead and waited for us.

I felt excited and a little important but this was quickly dispelled by the peremptory manner in which I was bundled into the back seat of the car. We drove in silence to the town of Zwolle and drew up outside the town hall. I was shepherded in through the front entrance into a hall filled with soldiers and civilians. After being searched I faced a barrage of questions, in answer to which I gave my name, rank and number: Sergeant Pilot Derek Thrower, RAF Number 904944. The interrogation over, I was taken upstairs and thrust into a room already occupied by three members of my crew. The front-gunner and rear-gunner were missing.

I was surprised and saddened that the four of us had been rounded up so quickly and so easily, but also relieved that they were safe and well. We talked quietly about the way each of us had been captured, but when one of the crew spoke of the squadron I cautioned him to be quiet, for it was obvious that the guard on the door was listening attentively and knew English. The guard was most upset when one of the crew asked him, in English, how much longer we were to be kept in this small room, and he answered in English before he could check himself! A minute later the guard was taken away.

A soldier appeared in the doorway, camera in hand. Quickly he took photographs of us, while we grinned back at him or pulled faces. None of this worried him and he disappeared without any fuss over our behaviour, and I concluded that he had taken the photographs for his own benefit.

I was still uneasy, even though there were no guards in the room. We had been there too long, and I began to wonder if the room had been wired for sound. So we discussed with enthusiasm the personal habits of German soldiers and in particular Hitler himself, and sure enough, the door soon burst open and an irate officer accompanied by his subordinates, entered the room. Red in the face, he waved his arms and fists and bellowed loudly. We were hustled down the stairs and out on to the front steps of the town hall to wait for the transport that was to take us to our next destination. Beside the still raging officer I recognized the guard who had been taking photographs of us. Carried away by the excitement and the noise I interrupted the voluble officer and explained to him about the guard and the camera. He shouted for a translation and turning on the now pale-looking offender demanded the camera from him and gave it to me! I gave it back and replied that it was not mine and that I did not want it, whereupon on getting the translation he lost his temper and booted me down the steps.

We were driven to Amsterdam and for the first time in my life I found myself in gaol, in solitary confinement. It lasted seven days, during which I learned the reality of being a prisoner. In that week I also became aware that I could not accept confinement passively.

It was a welcome relief to be interrogated from time to time by a relay of men. The first visitor was a pleasant German who offered me a cigarette and lit it for me, then handed me what he described as a Red Cross form which had to be completed in full. This would then be sent to the Red Cross authorities in Switzerland, who in turn would pass the information to England, informing my parents that I was alive and well and a prisoner of war.

The form looked genuine enough. I filled in my name rank and number; but when I came to questions which asked for the number of my squadron, where it was located, what kind of planes were used on bombing missions, and many other questions relating to the same kind of information, I drew a line through the form and handed it back. He repeated that the questions must be answered before the form could be sent off, and reminded me of my family's anxiety about whether I was alive or dead. I replied that I understood my family's feelings better than he did and had given enough information to allay those feelings. He seemed sad, and said that the German authorities would be unable to send the form until I had filled in the details asked for.

My next visitor was an aggressive fellow who on entering the cell shouted at me to stand to attention. He waved a gun around, occasionally pointing it at me, all the while stamping and shouting and threatening that I would be shot if I did not fill in the form. I refused, and he disappeared still ranting away. The next day a fine handsome German officer appeared. He was gentle and refined and spoke English with an excellent accent. Introducing himself, he offered me a cigarette and threw a large packet of them on the bed saying that I could keep them. He went on to talk about England, what a pleasant country it was, and how he had spent many years studying in London. He had had a girlfriend when he was there and asked if I had one, and where did we go when we had a date. He was a clever man and seemed so perfectly innocuous that if I had not been on my guard I could easily have given him the information he wanted. Eventually I simply stopped answering him. He was not annoyed at my taciturnity, but he took the packet of cigarettes with him when he left.

My first visitor reappeared, and placed before me a Red Cross form filled in with all the information that the Germans had wanted from me. I was shocked by what I saw, but sat still and said nothing. He told me that there was no reason now not to fill in the form. They had got all the information they needed so it was now only a matter of routine. I remained still and silent until he left the cell taking the forms with him; and with his departure the interrogators went out of my life for the time being.

From Amsterdam, our first destination was Dulag Luft transit camp, on the outskirts of Frankfurt: the collection point from which RAF prisoners were dispersed into the hinterland of Germany. The first part of the journey was by covered lorry to Utrecht. From there we were to travel by train to Frankfurt.

We were given a strong escort of armed soldiers for the journey; we found out why outside the station at Utrecht, when the Dutch people in the locality realized that we were RAF prisoners. They milled around the escort, giving the V-sign and throwing cigarettes and chocolate to the prisoners, until the guards, fearful at being swamped by such numbers, threatened to shoot if the Dutch did not move away.

I was thrust into an empty carriage and left alone for a few minutes while the guards directed the remaining prisoners to other places on the train. The crowds had made their way onto the platform and were peering through the windows. It was good to get such encouragement from these people. I wound down the carriage windows a little, and immediately cigarettes and biscuits were flying into the carriage. With glee I shoved my arm through the opening and with two fingers I gave them the V-sign. There was a great cheer. When I repeated the gesture I received a stunning blow on the chin. I jumped to my feet in anger, my fists clenched, to come face to face with the officer in charge of the escort. He screamed at me like a maniac, punching and slapping me as he yelled. Behind him stood two guards with their rifles at the ready. I remained tense and motionless while he continued to shout at me in a high-pitched voice, his mouth working overtime in the midst of his red face. Finally, running out of steam, he slammed me back into my seat with his fist, closed the window and left. The guards remained, their rifles pointed at me. I had gone too far in my enthusiasm for my new-found allies, and I had not appreciated how frightened the escort was by the unexpectedly large crowds.

The train steamed out of the station, and gradually the tension evaporated and I could relax in my seat, while the guards sat down opposite, their rifles at their sides. I looked out of the window, and was enthralled by the sight of the Rhine flowing majestically on its way to the sea. For a man who had never been out of England before, the journey along the banks of the Rhine to Frankfurt was an unforgettable experience. The sun shone in a deep blue sky and the surface of the river glinted and flashed in its beams, furrowed by the tugs and barges pushing their way against the stream.

We reached Dulag Luft at nightfall, and once again I found myself alone in a cell. Once again I had my quota of visitors, pleading, beguiling, threatening—just fill in the form and all would be well. And if I did not—well, my captors were in no hurry. My clothes were taken away from me and I could have them back when I had done what I was asked. For three days the treatment went on, and though I did not feel as confident as I had at the start I still refused to answer their questions. My clothes were returned and I was bundled out into the main camp.

The few days I spent at Dulag Luft behind barbed wire, living with hundreds of other RAF aircrew prisoners of war of all ranks from Wing-Commander to Sergeant in over-crowded conditions, was a bewildering experience. My own crew apart, I knew nobody. Day and night the conversations hinged on introductions followed by explanations as to how one was shot down. The stories were legion and the sense of frustration and misery, mixed up with the excitement of what might have been, showed how desperately difficult these men were finding it to adjust to a new way of life. To be hunted down and captured and then penned in like cattle seriously disturbed many of them. The watch-towers around the perimeter of the camp patrolled by men and machine guns, the cramped confined space, the primitive conditions and the poor quality of the food all helped to confuse the mind.

It was a time of despair: the awful yearning for home, to wander along the lovely English lanes with their sweet smelling wild flowers made my nights a torment. A strong determination to escape grew steadily, though reason told me that I was raw and inexperienced and I must learn to know my enemy first.

In the midst of all this gloom there was light relief when a P.O.W. made an abortive attempt to escape. During daylight hours prisoners were allowed to use an adjoining field to play football. The field was surrounded by a high barbed-wire fence patrolled by guards. In a corner of the field was a wooden pen which housed a ferocious-looking goat with large horns. The goat was let out when the field was unoccupied, but on occasions when the P.O.W.s were a little laggardly in their movements to leave, the guards released the goat which immediately set off at high speed across the ground, galvanizing the men into instant action as the goat thundered towards them. The joke misfired one day when the goat decided to attack one of the guards instead. Hampered by his rifle and long greatcoat, the guard had little chance of making the gate before the goat hit him. The guard rose into the air like a swan from a lake, borne up by the cheers and laughter of the prisoners.

The P.O.W.'s plan to escape was to dive unseen into the pen at the very last minute in the hope that the guards might not check the pen when they let out the goat. But he reckoned without the goat, which took exception to such intrusion, and the banging and squealing could be heard all over the field. The guards unlocked the pen, and out shot the prisoner followed closely by the goat, head down and highly enraged. The fleeing P.O.W. escaped back to solitary confinement, where he was allowed several days to nurse his bruises and hurt pride.

Early one morning, a number of non-commissioned officers were called out of line. I was one of them. We were informed that we were to be transferred to Stalag IXc, a camp at Bad Sulza near Leipzig. We collected our few bits and pieces, lined up at the main gate and marched out, heavily escorted, to a small convoy of covered lorries, in which we embarked for our new destination.

2

Escape

Our first stop was to be the station in Frankfurt. We drove through the city. Once the guards had satisfied themselves that there was no chance of us escaping, they lined up by the tailboard, and pulling aside the tarpaulin that covered the back of the lorry, began calling out or whistling to the girls passing by, and making jocular remarks to each other. Ginger, the wireless operator from my crew, in a moment of aberration expertly lifted a bayonet from its sheath and slid it into his battledress. The owner was busy making eyes at the girls and remained unaware of his loss, until eventually the convoy drew up in a siding—and the guards at the order jumped down, unslung their rifles and fixed bayonets! Pandemonium broke out, and at a command rifles were brought up at the ready and the bolts rammed home. It required no further persuasion for Ginger to hand over the bayonet and the tension eased at once, though we were hustled a little vigorously into the train.

There were some fifty P.O.W.s and these were allocated one carriage, with another for the guards, the two coupled together in the middle of a chain of wagons. Our carriage was of the open variety with seats facing each other and a table in between. The windows were shut and all of them had been securely screwed down. There were no curtains. Down the centre of the carriage ran a gangway, along which guards were placed at intervals. The remainder of the guards returned to their own carriage through a communicating door, and we were left to make ourselves as comfortable as we could on the hard wooden seats, and look out at the changing countryside as the train rattled into motion on its journey to Leipzig.

Hour after hour the train clattered away, stopping sometimes in a siding to let the faster trains by, at other times dropping off a few wagons and collecting new ones; then back onto the main line to continue its journey. In the mid-afternoon the rations appeared: bread, margarine and *leberwurst*, and a blunt dinner knife, produced reluctantly in response to our request for something to cut the bread with. One member of the group was given the job of distributing the rations, a long slow task.

While waiting for my share I obtained permission from the nearest guard to use the toilet. At the far end of the carriage, another guard, standing by the closed toilet door, indicated to me to wait. In a glass panel on the wall was a small map of Germany: with difficulty I found both Frankfurt and Leipzig and I tried to estimate on the map where we might be at that moment. I came upon Switzerland at the bottom of the map, and for a few moments I indulged in daydreams of a successful escape, and the excitement of crossing the frontier to freedom.

The guard signalled that I could go in. Once inside, I closed the door, but as there was no bolt I could not lock it. What light there was came from a frosted window pane above which was a small fanlight also of frosted glass, securely screwed down. In the corner by the window was the lavatory, with a pipe running up the wall to a small cistern near the ceiling; beside it was a washbasin with a cupboard underneath. I looked inside —empty. On the fanlight I counted six screws fastening it to the frame. It was the usual oblong shape, and not a large fanlight.

An absurd idea flashed into my mind. I had been in that toilet for some two minutes already, and the guard had made no move to open the door and look in. The question in my mind was whether I could get through the fanlight. It certainly looked impossible, but in my excitement at the thought of escaping nothing now was impossible. Without any further thought I made up my mind to try. I went back into the carriage—the guard outside still seemingly uninterested in my coming and going—and moved down the gangway to the table where the prisoner delegated to sharing out our rations was still busy. Portions of bread and *leberwurst* littered the table, and in the midst of it lay the knife.

While I collected my rations from him I outlined rapidly my plan of escape. I knew I would need help from the other P.O.W.s, and asked him to arrange for them to go in turn at decent intervals to the toilet with the bread knife secreted in their battledress. They were to go in, close the door, take out the knife and use it as a screwdriver to loosen the screws in the fanlight. Nobody was to stay in the place for longer than two minutes. When the job was done he was to let me know.

Without any change of expression he told me to clear off and leave it to him. I slipped back to my seat and chewed away at the bread and *leberwurst*, my heart thumping away with fear and excitement at the thought of the action I was going to take.

Afternoon dragged on into evening and nothing seemed to be happening. It was dark outside and the lights had been switched on in the carriage. The guards were changed and the new ones looked sharp and suspicious. I became tense and nervous and when somebody slipped into the seat beside me I leapt like a scalded cat. It was the dispenser of rations, who informed me that all the screws had been taken out except two and they were loose and easy to unscrew. In the cupboard under the washbasin he had placed a portion of bread and a tin of cigarettes; he thought I might need them. The mention of cigarettes amused me momentarily for I had never enjoyed a cigarette, only a pipe. If only to reassure myself that all was well I took it out of my pocket now and clamped it between my teeth. At this moment I needed some reassurance, for in planning to escape I had in fact planned nothing; only the urge to escape had filled my mind. He wished me luck and slipped quietly back to his seat, while I sat staring into the distance, my mind in a chaotic state as I tried to determine what my next move would be, and the next, and the next.

Several minutes later I was still in my seat. I needed courage, and I had little of it at that moment. Once I left my seat there would be no turning back. Instinctively I felt that every eye was watching me and I became aware of a building-up of tension in the carriage.

Suddenly everything was resolved. The voice of the interpreter could be heard above the noise of the train. He was telling us that we would arrive at Bad Sulza within the hour, and that we must start getting ready. It had to be now.

I walked down the gangway. The guard stood aside as I entered the toilet and closed the door. Within seconds I had taken out the two screws, lifted the fanlight out and placed it on the floor, leaving the screws tidily on top of the glass. Inside the cupboard I found the cigarettes and bread, and these I placed inside my jacket.

At that moment the train rushed into a tunnel, the noise reverberating around the tiny compartment so loud to my ears that I thought the guard outside must surely open the door to see what was going on. Nothing happened. I realized that I was holding my breath, and let it out.

It was time for me to go, but immediately the problem of making my exit through the narrow fanlight on a train that was now rushing through the night seemed an insuperable task. To go out head-first was the simplest method, and had the virtue of resolving all my problems the moment I made my exit. The alternative was to make my exit feet first, but how? I was still wearing my pyjamas under my battledress uniform, and the bulging outlines of the lump of bread and the tin of cigarettes and my large flying boots showed me what additional problems lay in wait as I tried to slip through the narrow aperture. To be stuck half in and half out of a moving train was a possibility I dared not think about.

With a sudden resolve I grasped the pipe leading up to the cistern, then lying back to the full extent of my arms and praying fervently that the piping would not give way I began to walk up the side of the carriage. With bent knees I laboriously placed one foot in front of the other until I was horizontal to the floor. Then, as the train swayed ominously. I pushed first one foot through the opening, then the other, and with a heave of my arms I slid through to find myself outside the train hanging precariously by one hand to the ledge of the window.

For a few moments I was blinded by the darkness. The wind battered my face, stinging my eyes and bringing tears to them, while at the same time it ripped through my clothes. My body banged again and again against the carriage as the train swayed and jolted over the lines. I bent my head to shield my eyes from the wind and stared down at the track below. To my horror I could see a twin set of lines running parallel to the track the train was on. I was on the inside of the track! In my mind's eye I could see the countless sleepers embedded in the stones below and I wondered which of them I would strike my head on—that is, of course, if I did not spatter my brains out on the line itself, or fall under the wheels of the train. But there was no longer any choice. I could not clamber back inside the coach, neither would I be able to hang on much longer, for the strain on my arm was causing the metal edge of the fanlight to cut into my fingers. Peering up at the opening I fully expected to see the guard's face looking at me, to be followed by the barrel of his rifle as he took aim. It would be impossible for me to explain that after all I did not want to escape, just to get back into the carriage. He would not understand English; in any case in the awful howling wind that battered my body against the train he would not be able to hear me. He would probably just shoot me.

Somehow I still held on, praying that the train would slacken speed, but it paid no heed to my prayers. With fear in my heart I prepared to let go. At the last moment I realized that my pipe was still clenched between my teeth, and with my free hand I jammed it into my jacket alongside the bread and cigarettes. Then, pedalling my feet furiously as though riding a bicycle, in the vain hope that I would be able to remain upright as I hit the ground, I took a deep breath and let go.

For a few frantic moments I was catapulting down the track, rolling over and over and over. The clattering wheels filled my ears with sound, and the flash of metal seared my eyes and then, suddenly, there was nothing.

I came to, to find myself sprawled between the tracks, my face burning and my back bruised and aching. For a time I lay there trying to understand what had happened, until my senses returned and I knew that I was alive and I was free. Sitting up I gazed up at the stars shining and twinkling in a clear night sky. The air was sweet and warm and my world was filled with a beautiful silence. It was a wonderful moment.

With enormous care I stood up, and with equal care I tested my limbs. Nothing was broken; just a few bruises, and a burning face. I clambered over the lines and buried my head in the cool wet grass at the side of the track. The burning stopped. I sat down and ferreted in my jacket for my pipe. It had gone, and so had the bread, but the cigarettes were still there. As I had no matches they were of little value to me at that moment!

A sound as though of footsteps broke the silence and my blood seemed to freeze. The only thought in my mind was that a search party had been sent out to look for me. I lay motionless and listened, but the sounds had disappeared. Suddenly it was urgent to get away from there. From a sighting of the Pole Star, and using the hands on my watch, I took a bearing; then quietly slipping over the lines and climbing down the bank I set off across the fields in a southerly direction. Ahead, and some hundreds of miles away, lay Switzerland.

3

On The Run

Being on the run is not for the nervous. Every sound one hears causes the heart to palpitate, and every shape that looms up out of the night takes on the figure of a human being, the enemy. My first hour of freedom was filled with such alarms. In front of me now lay a river, fast flowing between the dark shadows of trees that lined each bank. It had to be crossed, but in what direction should I follow the river to find a bridge, east or west? Instinctively I turned westwards and moved along the river bank. Within minutes I found what I was seeking, for ahead of me, inviting and welcoming, stood a bridge. Delighted with myself I stepped onto the bridge—only to freeze in my tracks at the sound of voices, voices so near that if I put out my hand I was sure I would touch somebody. Two men, their bodies merging into the darkness of the wall, were leaning over the parapet gazing down at the water flowing beneath, and talking quietly to each other. On the far side stood a large building, light pouring from its lower windows. Slowly, gently, I lowered myself into a crouching position and moved backwards off the bridge. It was astonishing to me that I had not been noticed; I must have been moving like a cat, nervous and taut as I was, and they too engrossed in their conversation to see me. Keeping down, I moved on past the bridge and along the bank.

After a while I began to hear the sound of rushing water, faintly at first, but increasing in volume as I moved on. In the faint light of the stars I saw the water tumbling over the edge of a weir and cascading into the darkness below.

Without thinking, intent only on getting across the river, I began to crawl along the top of the weir on all fours, the water curling and hissing around my legs and hands. Inch by inch I grasped my way forward. My clothes were quickly soaked through by the cascading water, which as I moved further away from the bank, gathered its strength to pluck me off my precarious perch and throw me into the cauldron below. I stopped. The idea that I could cross the river by such a method was preposterous. Step by step I retreated, until with sheer relief I tumbled backwards onto the bank. Lying there in my wet clothes, my limbs numbed by the water, it seemed to me that the methods I was using to make my escape were becoming more and more scatter-brained and increasingly dangerous. I must pull myself together.

I set off back to the bridge. The lights in the building were out now, and though I listened for some time, I could not hear voices or the sound of any movement. Quietly, on tiptoe, I crept over the bridge, past the darkened building, clambered over a wooden fence, darted across a lane and once more found myself in open country.

I trudged on over fields and ditches, occasionally slipping across a lane or road and back into the fields again, stopping now and then to take my bearings and moving on, keeping always to the fields. My eyes were accustomed to the darkness, and though I was tired from my strenuous activities I felt more relaxed and confident. That is until, without warning, the skyline was filled with the silhouettes of houses. They looked dark and menacing, for where there were houses there were people. My body told me that it had no intention of skirting round them, so after some hesitation I moved forward in between them. The houses grew thicker and closer together and I found myself in a narrow winding street.

A cough from an open upstairs window stopped me in mid-step. Close by a dog barked loudly in the stillness. Motionless, my breath drawn in, I stood trying to pierce the darkness surrounding the houses, looking for the blurred shape of a figure at a window. Blessedly, the barking stopped. With great care I pulled off my flying boots and, tucking them under my arm, I tiptoed through the village until I reached the safety of the open fields on the far side. Under a bush in a small copse at the edge of a field I curled up like a dog and fell asleep.

I woke to the sound of birds. The day was warm and bright and the countryside looked very English. In the next field a labourer was hoeing the ground contentedly. As I stretched out in the long grass, my hands behind my head, the events of the past twenty-four hours took on a dream-like quality in my mind. Here, lying in the sun luxuriating in its warmth, I might have been out in the field at home. Yet as my mind relived the incidents that had taken place I felt excited at what I had accomplished; with it came an impatience to be on my way, an impatience I knew I had to quell. I felt hungry too.

The day passed slowly but I remained under cover, not bold enough yet to move about in the daylight. I dozed under the hot sun, waking suddenly to any unfamiliar sound. At last the sun dropped down behind the trees, and in the twilight I set off across the fields. It was rough travelling, for my feet were blistering and my limbs ached from the exertions of the night before.

Before me lay a scattering of houses; lights glowed from windows, evocative of crackling fires and tables laden with rich foods. Hypnotized by such visions I stepped inside a gate and peered vainly through a crack in the curtains. The sound of footsteps sent me rushing out into the fields, where I cowered listening for the sound of pursuit.

Chastened by my stupidity I went on my way, avoiding the houses, moving steadily southwards. A wooden fence barred my way. This I climbed, and landing on the other side I rolled down a steep grassy embankment. Quite by accident I had come upon one of Germany's famous autobahns. I remembered reading that pedestrians were not allowed on these roads. This one was leading in the direction I wanted to go, and, in the knowledge that I was safe from any human intrusion I marched off along the road. It was better going now and I relaxed into an easy rhythm of walking.

The sound of a car behind me sent me rushing headlong onto the grass verge. I flattened myself in the long grass as it raced by, its headlamps lighting up the road ahead of it. I lay still for a while enjoying the rest, and it was with reluctance that I got to my feet and continued my journey. This time I stayed close to the verge, ready to leap back into the grass at the sound of an engine.

The road began to slope steeply upwards. I walked on, alert for any sound. Suddenly the deep throbbing of a hard-working engine sent me flailing into the verge. I craned my neck above the grass to watch the approaching lights of the vehicle below as it growled its way up the hill. It lost momentum on the steep gradient and I heard the grating sound of changing gears as it passed by. It was a heavy open lorry, pulling a four-wheeled trailer behind it.

The lorry had now slowed down to almost a walking pace. An idea crossed my mind; no sooner there than I acted on it, jumping to my feet and padding after the lorry as hard as my tired limbs could go. Reaching it, I leapt up and grabbed the top of the tailboard of the trailer, swung my leg upwards and over, and with a wild grab caught hold of a wooden container and hauled myself on to the trailer.

It was loaded with wooden crates, full of long-necked empty wine bottles clacking and ringing in time with the rhythm of the lorry. In a space by the tailboard a sack of potatoes stood, nestling among the crates. The lorry had now gathered speed and as it bumped along the crates hopped up and down and I hopped up and down with them. It was an uncomfortable way to ride, and I clambered over to the sack of potatoes and mounted it like a jockey on his steed, my knees bent on either side of the sack and gripping it like a vice; and so I rode with my back to the tailboard, my hands clutching the crates in front of me to prevent myself from falling off onto the road.

Perched as I was I could see quite clearly through the cabin window of the lorry the silhouettes of the driver and his mate. No matter how much I tried to flatten myself against the potatoes I was sure that if they bothered to look back carefully they would be able to see me outlined above the crates. However, I could always jump off before the lorry stopped and slip away in the darkness.

The lorry roared on into the night. I became accustomed to the movement, though my position was precarious and I might easily be tossed off the trailer if I relaxed for a moment. To make myself more secure, I leaned forward over the sack and, stretching one arm as far as it could go over the crates, I jammed two fingers into the necks of wine bottles and clutched the potatoes with the other arm.

I must have fallen asleep, for I woke to find myself bathed in the glare of headlamps as a car raced up behind the lorry and overtook it at great speed. Instinctively I glanced up at the cabin, to see the white face of the driver's mate peering through the window.

He could not fail to see me, so strongly outlined in the beams of the oncoming car.

The car passed without slackening speed, but the lorry immediately began to draw up by the side of the road. Conscious of the staring eyes, I rose from the sack to find that my two fingers were jammed in the necks of the bottles. I could not release them! With my feet on the tailboard and the two bottles wedged against the crate I struggled to free them but without success. The lorry stopped, the doors of the cab swung open violently, and out jumped the two men. The ignominy of being caught with two wine bottles dangling from my fingers gave me the strength I needed. With one final wrench my fingers popped from the bottles and twisting in mid-air I jumped over their groping hands, landing like a cat on hands and feet. Before they could move I was on my feet again and running off into the darkness. Their hesitation was only a split second, and I could hear the clumping of their boots on the road close behind me.

My cramped muscles slowed me down and the flying boots made running awkward. I sensed that my adversaries were gaining on me and it would be a matter of seconds before I was caught. In a desperate gamble I put all my energy into a wild burst of speed, gaining two or three valuable yards on them. Almost as suddenly I veered sharply away and stood still. The two men, dark shapes in the night, flew past me. Ducking down I tiptoed on to the grass verge and waited, crouching low in the grass. The men halted, muttering to each other, then, quickly running back to their lorry, they drove off.

It was time for me to hole up and rest. Not far from the autobahn I came upon a wood. I soon found some bushes, and crawling into the middle of them I curled up and fell asleep.

It was early dawn when I woke from a sound sleep.

The sky was cloudless, and the air at that early hour was cool and fresh. I did not feel the hunger of the day before and I was eager to be on my way. There was a new confidence in my attitude to being on the run and I entertained no thoughts of remaining under cover till nightfall. I argued with myself that if I behaved normally the people I came across would not be suspicious of me. In my exuberence and *naïveté* I was not fully aware of the strange figure I would present to anyone I met! My hair was untidy and dirty, my face unshaven, my uniform was creased and stained and I was wearing a dirty pyjama jacket as a shirt. My flying boots, now sagging at the sides, were not the kind of footwear that men usually wore, and to complete the picture I was still wearing my pilot's brevet and my sergeant's stripes.

I pulled my trouser legs over the top of my flying boots and ripped off the stripes from my jacket. As for my brevet, it was too precious to me to discard it and I thought I could hide it from the gaze of any curious person by holding the lapel of my jacket with my left hand.

In any case, to stay on or near the autobahn during daylight was dangerous, so I set off across country, still on a heading that was roughly south. It was not long before I came to the edge of a forest. There was less chance of meeting strangers by keeping in its shelter and I was soon weaving my way through the trees. At first the going was easy but as the sun rose in the sky the humidity in the forest made me hot and uncomfortable, and I longed for a drink. My socks were creasing under my feet and blistering them. It was easy for me to lose my sense of direction. I stopped frequently to check the position of the sun and it was with a sense of relief that I broke out of the trees into a clearing.

I sat down in the grass and took off my boots and socks to cool my feet; the soles were badly blistered. I stretched out my legs, and looked around. To east and west the clearing stretched as far as the eye could see. It was a fire break. Above the trees a watch-tower was visible, used presumably to pin-point the outbreak of a forest fire. Through the middle of the clearing ran a dirt track, and as my eyes followed it into the distance I saw approaching me a workman on his bicycle.

I began pulling on my socks again, trying to decide what action I should take. He was close to me by now and slowing down, curious about the stranger sitting in the grass without his boots and socks. I jumped to my feet and, waving a boot at him, I shouted, "*Guten Morgen.*" Which of us was the more frightened would be hard to tell, for he immediately pressed down on his pedals and wobbled away down the track, turning his head again and again. Each time he turned I waved my boot at him until, gauging that he was now far enough away, I pulled on my boots and ran off into the trees.

As I struggled on, hour after hour, through the forest, the air grew hot and sticky. Sweating profusely, I sought protection from hordes of horse-flies that attacked my face and hands. Though I covered my head with my jacket, they found their way under it, biting me again and again. There was no relief from them. My lips were parched but I could find no water to drink.

All the tracks I came across seemed to run in an east-west direction. I was determined to keep on course and felt that the forest must come to an end soon—I could not rest because of the horse-flies.

Shortly after midday I scrambled down a steep bank into a hollow. A small stagnant pool of water covered in green scum lay at the bottom. Creaming off some of the slime I ducked my head into the water and drank greedily. The water tasted brackish and bitter, but I felt better. Climbing out of the hollow I continued my journey. An hour later I was as parched and hot as before.

It was mid-afternoon when I stumbled exhausted out of the forest. Below me lay a wide valley of green meadows and yellow fields of corn. Through them meandered a young stream, cool and inviting, and close by, a road ran down the valley, disappearing into a cluster of tiny cottages that stood mellow and warm in the sun. I could hear the voices of young children as they played, and dotted over the valley men and women were working in the fields.

Perhaps I should have remained where I was until nightfall, but I was desperately thirsty. At the same time I needed a rest badly. My feet were in poor shape, my body cried out for water, and it was a long time since I had eaten any food. The valley was welcoming and innocent and I felt no sense of danger in joining in the life that flowed below. I picked out a spot on the far bank of the stream, close by a footbridge, where a cluster of small trees and bushes grew close to the bank and hid it from the road.

Using a branch for support, I moved through the fields down into the valley. The sun was still strong but the air was cool and pleasant. The horse-flies had disappeared. I crossed the road and made my way over the footbridge. The water was ice-cold. I drank greedily, then bathed my face and hands, and oblivious to any thoughts of discovery I took off my boots and socks and sat happily on the bank, dangling my feet in the stream. Above, on the slopes, I could hear children calling out to each other.

I sat in the sun until my hands and feet had dried, then pulled on my socks and boots. The need to sleep became overpowering, and I crawled under the nearby bushes and closed my eyes.

The sound of voices hammered in my ears, and I woke up startled to see a group of men, women and children standing on the other side of the stream watching me—the men silent and curious, the children calling excitedly. The children must have seen me, and attracted the attention of the others. Among the group were two or three young men. They were the danger. In my present condition they would have no difficulty in overpowering me. Somehow I had to get away before they came to any decision about what to do.

I stood up slowly and deliberately, picked up my staff, then turned and faced them, smiled as charmingly as I could, and said in my best German, *"Guten Tag"*. It was my hope that they would think that I was an eccentric old tramp! With a wave of my staff I turned away and began to walk slowly and carefully up the slope of the valley towards the plateau above. My heart was thumping, and I had the strongest desire to run for my life. The children were shouting more loudly than ever and I turned and waved to them and continued my slow uphill climb. Every few steps I took I turned back to see what action the group was taking, trying to delay the decision they might make by waving happily to them each time.

Nearing the top of the slope I looked back again. The crowd was splitting up and two younger men were already crossing the bridge and climbing the slope. They were coming at walking pace, and though I was beginning to feel afraid I continued to walk. Gratefully I reached the top. The moment I was out of sight I ran. Away to my left was a wood, and I raced into it. Without looking back I ran on and on until I could run no longer. Mercifully there was no sound of pursuit, and after regaining my breath I moved on again.

The countryside was beautiful in the afternoon sun. I made my way through meadows and cornfields until, as the sun sank low in the sky, I came to a narrow lane bending its way down a hillside. A brook ran alongside bordered by a wild overgrown hedge. Crossing the lane

I jumped the brook and scrambled through the hedge into the field beyond, and stretched full-length in the grass. It was wonderful to be alive and still free.

Sitting up, I opened the tin of cigarettes before I remembered that I had no matches. I knew that boy scouts would not be put off by such circumstances, and gathering some twigs I faithfully rubbed two of them against each other. To no avail, though my fingers grew hot from the exercise and the friction.

Taking off my boots and socks, I slid back through the gap in the hedge and bathed my feet in the brook. Two cyclists rode down the hill, a man with a lovely young woman as his companion. They were calling out to each other as they pedalled along, but broke off, disconcerted, and stopped pedalling as they came upon me standing barefoot in the brook. They coasted towards me, silent and curious, while I stood taut and nervous, one foot half out of the water. The girl suddenly laughed aloud, and with a wave of her hand called out a greeting. The man followed her example and I waved back happily as they pedalled down the lane laughing at each other.

Just before dark I came upon the autobahn again, winding its way southwards through the countryside. I followed it until the road began to climb. Half-way up the slope a concrete bunker of sand stood in the middle verge. I retired into a nearby field to rest until it was dark.

The sky had grown overcast, rain began to fall. I looked for a place to shelter and using a small tree with branches close to the ground, I gathered sticks and shrubs to make a hide-away that would withstand the rain. In this I was more successful than I had been when trying to make fire, and pleased with myself, I crept into my lair as a badger or a fox would do. It was warm and snug and dry and I promptly fell asleep.

The time by my watch was two in the morning and I was angry with myself for sleeping so long. I hurried back to the autobahn and crouched down beside the sand bunker, still cursing myself for wasting valuable hours of darkness. There would be little or no traffic at such a late hour, and I could be stuck there for hours.

In the midst of these reflections I heard the sound I wanted to hear, the rumble of a heavy vehicle as it ground its way up the hill towards my hiding-place. I crouched down behind the bunker as it roared slowly past, then jumped out on the road and chased after it. The vehicle by now was moving at a slow running pace as it reached for the top of the rise, and I jogged alongside looking for a place to get a foothold.

To my dismay it was a large pantechnicon, smooth and box-like, with a trailer of the same kind. I examined the coupling between the lorry and the trailer, two iron bars attached to the trailer and coupled together at the rear of the lorry so that it looked like a large V-sign.

The lorry was gathering speed. Reluctant to lose the chance of a lift I jumped in between the wagons and vaulted on to one of the bars, settling myself sideways as though riding a horse side-saddle, at the same time grasping both bars firmly to secure myself against any jolts or turns.

Within moments the lorry was racing away along the flat and it was all that I could do to keep my balance and keep my feet up away from the ground. Every bump on the road sent me skywards, and only the strong grip I had on the round bars prevented me from being thrown under the wheels. The wind tore through the gap between the wagons, ripping through my clothes, and whipping my hair into my eyes. The cold violence of the wind chilled my body and the constant jolting bruised my thighs. My arms and wrists ached as I held on grimly.

Without slowing up the lorry turned off the autobahn

and thundered through the night along narrow twisting roads, through villages and towns. Some of the bends in the road that the driver had to negotiate were so acute, I thought that at the speed he was going the wagons would jack-knife. As it was, I was in danger of being crushed as the corners of the wagons closed together.

The road surfaces were far worse now that we had left the autobahn and the strain of hanging on became well-nigh intolerable. My hope was that at one of the bends the lorry would slow up sufficiently for me to slip off, but as time passed I knew that such an attempt would be suicidal. Stiff and sore as I was, and numb from cold, I would not be fast enough to clear the wheels in time. So I hung on and hoped that I would survive.

For three more hours I hung on while an unseen driver frantically pursued his nightmare journey to an unknown destination. At Saalfeld the journey ended, outside the railway station. The rushing wind and the noise disappeared. Painfully, I unclenched my hands and fell onto the road; then fearfully, in case he should drive off again, I crawled towards the pavement on my hands and knees. As I crept out from between the wagons the driver jumped down from his cab. The apparition he saw so unnerved him that he fell against the lorry, staring stupidly, his mouth open. I hauled myself upright, turned my back on him and hobbled away.

My watch showed just after 5 a.m. The dawn was misty and grey, for which I was grateful. As I made my way through the town I was passing many people on their way to work. I knew that I must look a grim sight after so horrifying a journey and I was thankful for the cover the semi-darkness gave me. As I walked the blood began to circulate again, painfully, through my body; and painful though it was, I was relieved to feel my limbs loosening up and my body warming up from the exercise of walking. I began to feel human again.

Saalfeld was a big town and it took me some while to reach the outskirts. It was growing lighter. Beyond the houses I could see the distant slopes of hills. I was beginning to feel more cheerful. Lengthening my stride I turned a corner into another street. Just fifty yards ahead of me stood a German policeman, gun in holster, one hand hooked in his belt as he looked down the street towards me. I was the only person in that street beside himself, and there was nothing to distract his attention. There was no alternative but to keep on walking towards him. I clutched the lapel of my jacket to hide the fact that I was still wearing my brevet.

Ten yards was all the distance between us now, and he had not once moved his gaze from me. That he was suspicious of me was obvious, yet I had to bluff it out. I just kept walking, right past him, ignoring him as though he was not there. His eyes followed me, his face showed that he was puzzled but did not know what to do. Ahead of me was a side turning. I kept walking at a steady pace and turned the corner without looking back. Just across the road was a narrow alleyway: the moment I was out of sight I bolted down it. It was a certainty that he would follow me, that he would make up his mind to question me. If I was not there, there was nothing he could do. I ran until I reached open country, panting, exhausted and hungry.

Ahead of me was an unmade road with a few houses straggling along one side of it, the gardens separating the houses from the road. As I passed along the bottom of one of the gardens I noticed in it rows of bushes full of delicious ripe raspberries. Glancing upwards at the windows of the house I saw that the curtains were closed. The inhabitants were probably asleep. I crept quietly through a little wicket gate and began to feast on the fruit. After days without food, the taste of the raspberries was a delight to my palate and I crammed them into my mouth as fast as I could pluck them from the bushes.

I was aware of a movement at one of the windows and instinctively crouched down where I stood, still plucking at the raspberries; then, as though shot from a bolt, I sped through the gate and up the lane as fast as my weary legs could carry me. There was no commotion behind me, and I slowed down and began to walk.

Without warning a clap of thunder reverberated across the sky and within seconds the rain lashed down. I looked for shelter. A short distance away lay a vegetable garden enclosed by a wire fence. Inside stood two outbuildings, like toolsheds. I vaulted over the wire and examined the first, to find it locked. I was luckier with the second: the place was cramped and uninviting, but it was shelter. Leaving the door open I sat down on a heap of earth inside and gazed out at the rain.

It was a violent storm, the thunder and lightning almost continuous, the clouds thick and black while the heavy and relentless rain poured down hour after hour. I sat bored and impatient, tired and damp. I was safe enough, for nobody would be foolish enough to walk out in such a downpour. My feast of raspberries had done little to temper the pangs of hunger I felt; indeed, the rumbles that went on in my stomach were loud enough to make me thankful there was nobody around to hear them.

Early in the afternoon the rain lessened and finally stopped. The clouds broke up and scattered and the sun appeared cheerful and warm. I stood up in my little shelter, smoothed the wrinkles in my damp trousers and brushed away the earth still sticking to them. I wanted to be on my way into the hills I had seen earlier, for they would be less populated and it would be safer for me to be on the move, particularly in daylight.

A few yards away on the other side of the fence a brook ran fiercely along the side of a sloping field. It had overflowed its banks and was now a miniature torrent racing down the slope towards a village at the bottom of the valley. Just beyond the brook a small copse of bushes grew, full of ripe raspberries. I could not resist the temptation to eat them, and clambering over the wire I jumped across the brook and savoured the juiciness of them in my mouth. Gradually I pushed into the centre of the bushes as I picked away at the fruit in an attempt to rid myself of the pangs of hunger.

Voices! I dropped down into the bushes, peering out to see from where the sounds were coming. To my dismay there were six men coming towards my hiding-place, shovels over their shoulders. They had been too busy talking to each other to have noticed me, but they were now too close for me to break out of the bushes and make my escape. I flattened myself to the ground and hoped fervently that they would not see me.

To my horror they stopped a few feet from the bushes and threw down their spades. For a few moments I was unnerved, but resisted the impulse to jump up and run. Instead I watched them, my body tense with fear. I could not understand why I could see them so clearly yet they could not see me. They stood as a group, watching the water cascading down the slope, talking among themselves. Now and then one or other would gesticulate with both hands, or point to the village. With sudden apprehension I knew that their purpose in coming to that spot was to divert the water into the field, to prevent flooding in the village below. If I was right, they were going to be around for some considerable time, and the chances of being discovered were high.

As if to confirm my thoughts, they turned as one man, moved up to the bushes, and taking off their jackets laid them on top. I could see each of their faces clearly as they bent over me. Three of them were strong young men, two men were middle-aged, and the sixth was an old man with most of his teeth missing. They turned back to the brook, picked up their spades and began to dig away at the bank. I had been given a temporary reprieve.

I dared not move. The slightest action would attract attention. All I could do was to lie still and hope that my luck would hold. For hours I lay on the damp grass while they toiled and talked, stopping only to wipe the sweat from their foreheads or straighten their backs. Slowly they channelled their way into the field, and the water spewed onto the grass, gently at first, then faster, until the area around the brook looked like a lake. I was thankful I was hidden upfield of the workers.

Their work finished, they stood back, and with varying grunts of satisfaction, surveyed the scene. They were pleased with themselves and the number of "*Ja*"s they mouthed to each other showed they were in complete accord about the success of their efforts. One after the other, the workers collected their jackets from the bushes above me, then turned away and picked up their spades—all except the old man. He stood facing the bushes as he put on his jacket and, like me, saw the raspberries. As soon as he had dressed he began to pick them one by one and put them in his mouth. I watched him above me, munching away, his mouth opening and shutting mechanically, while red saliva ran down his chin.

Pushing further into the bushes, he stretched out his hand and stopped, frozen in mid-action. He had seen me. I lay motionless, full-stretch on the ground as his eyes travelled up my body till they reached my face. His eyes widened in astonishment and fear, his mouth full of fruit slowly opened and his arm outstretched above me remained rigid. We stared at each other, transfixed for what seemed an eternity.

My brain began to work again. I was frightened and helpless, and lying on my back, in the worst possible position to make good my escape. With a suddenness that left him even more afraid than I was, though it showed only on his face, I jumped to my feet. My next action I could not account for unless it was auto-suggestion. Raising a hand to my face, I mimed the idea of hunger by opening my mouth and pushing my fingers in and out of it. I then chewed my lips at the same time rubbing my stomach with my other hand. The only rational explanation I could think of as an excuse for such a ridiculous pantomime was that I needed time to work out what action I could take to avoid capture. It served only to make him confused and bewildered. He turned his head towards his companions who were talking to each other while they waited for him, unaware of the scene being played out before them.

As he turned away from me I sprang from the bushes and with a leap jumped the brook. Ahead of me lay a long sloping bank leading into a cornfield. Beyond were the hills and safety. Glancing back as I ran on, I saw that the enemy were splitting into two groups. Four of them strung out in a line were already chasing me while the other two were running towards the village.

I laboured up the slope into the cornfield. My flying boots, worn down from all the walking, were flapping on my feet. They were manifestly unsuitable for this kind of chase. Looking back over my shoulder I saw with sinking heart that two of the younger men were gaining on me. Desperate, I stopped, pulled off my boots and tucked them under my arm. The lead man caught up with me and grabbed my arm. I ducked and twisted, breaking his hold, and raced away down the track that divided the cornfield in two.

Fear gave me added strength, and free of the boots, my feet twinkled over the grass. I gained on my pursuers, and their shouts of anger and frustration sounded sweetly in my ears. Spurred on by my success in evading capture I ran faster than ever, and the gap between us slowly widened.

Away to my right, not very far away, were the hills I so wanted to reach. Between them and me was a wood that bordered on the cornfield. At the centre of the cornfield I came on another track at right angles to the one that I was in, leading straight down to the wood. Turning into it I saw that I was now some thirty yards ahead of my adversaries.

I ran on and on. My mouth was open as I gulped in large draughts of air to relieve my lungs. My legs were like rubber. A hedge loomed up, and with an effort I plunged headlong through it into the wood beyond, landing spread-eagled on the ground.

Scrambling to my feet I began to run again, only to stop suddenly. The wood was narrow at this point, and through the trees I could see a road running parallel to the wood, and beyond it a railway line. In the middle of the road stood a group of cyclists. Behind me I could hear the shouts of my pursuers. The noise they made had not yet penetrated through the trees to the group on the road, but it could only be a matter of seconds before they heard their cries.

Trapped! A feeling of helplessness swept through me. There was no place to hide. The trees were young and widely spread and there was little undergrowth around to hide in. History in the unlikely guise of King Charles II came to my rescue. Remembering that the King had hidden in a tree while the Roundheads were looking for him, I slipped on my boots again and examined the tree next to me. It was about twenty-five feet tall, with few branches, and few leaves on them except near the top. I began climbing the trunk as quickly as I could.

It was not a moment too soon, for I was still some way from the top when my pursuers crashed through the hedge into the wood and stopped below me. I clung motionless to the trunk not daring to breathe. Luckily, the first thing they saw were the cyclists on the road, and shouting and gesticulating they ran to meet them while I quickly climbed to the top. The trunk I was clinging to was of pole-like dimensions and as I hung on, my head half in, half out through the leaves, the wind caused it to sway to and fro rather alarmingly.

The two parties joined forces and spread out in a line across the width of the wood. I watched, grinning through my teeth as they passed below, peering into the sparse undergrowth, and moving on. If one of them had thought of looking up into the trees he would have seen me. I felt a little hysterical as I swayed backwards and forwards in the strengthening wind.

A large raindrop splashed on my forehead, and as I looked up a clap of thunder vibrated across the sky. Large ominous-looking black clouds swirled above me, and it began to rain; slowly at first, then faster and heavier, it lashed the trees. Lightning ripped the clouds, and thunder followed fast and loud. The wind blew in a frenzy, and my perch began to resemble the rigging of some old timbered ship in a storm at sea.

Looking down through the leaves I could see the men below still searching the wood, and hear the sound of a vehicle approaching. As I peered out at the road, a tarpaulin-covered lorry came into view from the direction of the village and pulled up alongside the heap of cycles at the side of the road. Twenty or more soldiers jumped out. With them I recognized the two members of the digging party who had run off in the direction of the village.

One of the party searching in the woods came running down the road. A rapid discussion followed, then a series of commands, at which the soldiers unslung their rifles, fixed beyonets, and doubled into the wood. Line abreast, their guns at the ready, they moved past below me at a steady pace, while I swayed to and fro above their heads.

This turn of events had shaken me. There was no

sense of fun in this. I was a hunted man. The sight of those menacing figures below began to terrify me: that, and the idea that a soldier, looking up and seeing me, would just raise his gun and fire. I felt weak, watching them anxiously as they moved away through the trees.

The rain was now thick and heavy, the wind roaring in gusts through the trees, while I swayed in an ever-increasing arc, wondering irrelevantly why babies did not get seasick in their cradles. I started to climb down, taking infinite care not to break any branches.

The sound of footsteps on the road froze my blood. I had been so busy watching the soldiers moving through the wood that I had not noticed the soldier left on duty to guard the lorry. From the bottom of the tree I watched him march up the road, then with a smart about-turn retrace his steps, all the while scanning the woods. I had been lucky that he had not seen me climbing down the tree.

As he stepped up the road with his back to me I slipped through the trees back towards the village. The Germans had not shown much originality in their thinking or tactics so far; they would not expect such a move. As the sentry turned about, I dropped to the ground and waited until he reached the end of his beat and marched back again. A few more yards and I had reached the end of the wood. Again I dropped to the ground, which was covered with surface water that ran through the grass onto the road below.

The earth seemed to tremble from the continuous thunder, and the lightning blinded my eyes, while rain ran through my hair and clothes. It was pure melodrama, a perfect setting in which to be hunted with the possibility of a killing at the end.

Forty yards away across an open field, stood a number of buildings, closely grouped together, and surrounded by a wooden fence some six feet high. If I could make my way over the field and climb the fence I might be safe from the enemy and perhaps find shelter from the storm. I turned back to watch the guard. He did not look so determined or wary as before. Already his shoulders were hunched and his head bent as he traced and retraced his steps.

As he turned away, I stood up and ran to the fence. It looked high, too high, but leaping for the top and pulling hard on my arms I succeeded in falling head first on to the other side, landing heavily on the squelchy ground. Winded but triumphant, I lay on my back while the rain splashed on my face.

I stood up. The state I was in would have compared unfavourably with a scarecrow. Water squelched out of my boots and a mixture of mud and water had melted into my clothes, while my face was grimy and unshaven. Physically I was exhausted. Hunger and a lack of sleep sapped my strength. A warm bed, a hot meal and a sympathetic nurse was what I needed.

From what I could see of it I was in a large garden adjacent to the buildings I had seen from the edge of the wood. Trees and shrubs dotted the place, and in the middle stood a wooden hut, its door ajar, inviting me to come in. I did so and found a room furnished with a couch, chairs and a table. I slumped gratefully on the couch.

Something was puzzling me, a sensation of movement around me. Focusing my eyes on the wall opposite me, I realized that it was constructed of glass, and so were the other walls. Behind the glass, bees in their thousands were swarming. I was in a gigantic beehive! There were bees everywhere, crawling on the floor, on the table and chairs, over the couch, and crawling over me. I rushed out of the door, slapping madly at my clothes to get rid of them. Looking for another place of shelter, I came upon an open gateway at the far end of the garden leading into a central courtyard surrounded by buildings. There were faces at the windows, looking out at the water swirling below as it rose inch by inch. Back in the garden, I found a piece of corrugated iron which I held over my head. Beside it were a number of bricks which I put together to form a platform high enough above the water level to allow me to sit on them.

The storm continued with a violence I had never seen before. I sat shivering, watching the water rise slowly until it covered the bricks and swirled through my trousers. Throwing away the shield over my head I moved to the entrance to the courtyard. Just inside, only a few feet away an open door led into an outhouse. Taking a chance of being seen from one of the windows I waded through the water and entered the building.

It was a wash-house. Clothes littered the floor and here and there stood a paraphernalia of boilers, sinks and scrubbing boards. In an attempt to warm myself, I burrowed into the clothes and lay there shivering and miserable.

Two men appeared in the doorway and stood there looking down at me. As I got to my feet, they came forward, one to either side of me, took hold of my arms, and propelled me through the door, across the flooded courtyard, and into the house.

I stood in the hallway, water from my clothes forming a pool on the floor. The place was jammed with people, young and old, gazing at me curiously and silently. I could only stare back, my senses dull with exhaustion. There was a movement in the crowd and a young girl, about seventeen, pushed her way to the front. She spoke in English. Though nervous and embarrassed she spoke gently and pleasantly. In reply to her questions I told her that I was English, that I was a prisoner of war and had escaped. She told me that they had been warned to keep a look-out for me, and that somebody in the house had already telephoned the police. As she spoke a sudden weakness caused me to stagger. Quickly she caught hold of my arm and steadied me. She spoke to somebody and a chair was found for me to sit on; then, taking a cigarette from someone's hand, she put it between my lips. A cup of coffee was placed in my hands and I drank the hot brew greedily. She asked me how old I was and why I was trying to escape, it was so dangerous. Others began to call out, asking questions which she translated for me. All around me were sympathetic faces.

The crowd stood aside as a policeman entered the door. He stood there, large, red-faced, gun in hand, water pouring off his clothes. I guessed that he had been out helping in the hunt for me. His foot shot out, kicking the chair from under me. As I sprawled on the floor, he kicked again and again until I was upright, then placing his boot in my back he sent me flying through the door face-first into the waterlogged courtyard, at the same time shouting and waving his gun. Climbing to my feet, I could see the girl on the doorstep, her face white and anxious. In my heart I was thankful I had met somebody decent. Another blow sent me staggering, followed by the jab of the gun in my back and the shout of a raucous voice in my ear.

As we marched out of the yard onto the road I was worried by the animosity of my captor, for I knew he wanted an excuse to shoot me. A military car drew up alongside and I was forced onto the floor face down. I remained still while the car drove off at a fast pace into Saalfeld. Within minutes I was standing in the outer office of the prison quarters in the army barracks.

A group of young soldiers wearing white flashes in their forage caps—officer cadets, in training—now surrounded me, come out of curiosity to see what their enemy looked like. They were eager young men, polite and pleasant. After the formalities of handing me over were completed I was given a seat. A lighted cigarette was thrust in my mouth and the cadets gathered round firing question after question. One cadet who spoke excellent English acted as interpreter. They had not seen any action so far and to them I looked truly a battle-scarred warrior. Eager to be involved in what I had been doing during my fighting career they would not be put off by my refusal to answer questions that I considered carried information helpful to the enemy.

We were interrupted by the arrival of the station adjutant. I saw that one side of his face was badly scarred. Every man in the room snapped to attention, remaining silent and still as he stood looking me up and down. He was clearly angry at the fraternization that had been going on, and at a sharp command I was bundled out of the room into a cell. The steel door was shut and I heard the key turning in the lock and bolts being shot home.

The cell was large and cold, with a wooden bench for a bed. There was no other furniture. A cell window high up in the wall was barred. The cold night air whistled through the bars and round the cell. There was little comfort for me in these quarters. I was surprised to find a cigarette still burning between my fingers. Foraging in my jacket I found my tin of cigarettes still intact. Taking one from the tin I lit it from the fag-end of the other; then removing my clothes I squeezed out the remaining water and put on my pyjamas again. They were cold and clammy against my skin. I pressed out my jacket and trousers and spread them on the floor; and then, clutching my tin of cigarettes, I lay back on the wooden bed. On into the night I lay shivering, smoking cigarette after cigarette until there were no more, finally falling asleep in the early hours of the morning.

The crashing sound of bolts being drawn woke me. The adjutant stood in the doorway, his face a mixture of contempt and disgust. Behind him his subordinates were peering over his shoulder. Standing up, I faced him, angry at this attempt to humiliate me. I could understand his disgust. Cigarette ends littered the floor, my pyjamas, stained by mud and water, were filthy, my face and hands were dirty and my hair matted with mud. But the contempt angered me, and strangely my anger gave me the upper hand. It upset him. He began to shout at me, and I felt happier, for the contempt had disappeared. Ignoring him, I began pulling on my clothes. He shouted louder, his voice breaking. Half-understanding his words, I guessed he was describing the kind of mess I was, and the state of the cell. Perversely this gave me pleasure, for he had lost his dignity and I had regained mine.

He stormed out of the cell. I stood listening as he visited the other cells, the doors opening and shutting with a boom, while in between, the adjutant, now thoroughly roused, screamed venomously at each inmate in turn.

For a while all was quiet, and then once more I heard the sound of cells doors being opened, and a continuous stream of shouted commands rang through the cells. The other prisoners were being taken out. Minutes later the shouting was taken up outside my cell window. I dragged the bed underneath the window, climbed up and looked through the bars. The prisoners, German soldiers being punished for some misconduct, were on the parade ground. Laden with packs and carrying rifles, they were running furiously backwards and forwards. At a command they would fall outstretched on their faces, then up again, running fast, only to have to fall again. This went on and on until tired and ashamed of such cruelty, I jumped down and paced up and down the cell.

The sun shone into my cell and warmed it. I dried out and felt more relaxed, though no food or water was given to me. I was left to myself without any further interruptions. When night came I stretched out and tried to sleep.

It was after midnight when I woke to find two soldiers standing beside the bed. One was a private, the other I recognized as the cadet who spoke such excellent English. He was wearing a greatcoat, and to my astonishment he pulled out from under it a bowl of thick gruel and a spoon. He told me to eat it and say nothing to anybody, or he would be in trouble. An order had been given that I was not to have any food, and he thought that it was unreasonable. As I ate he spoke to me of his studies in Heidelberg, the friends he had made, both English and American and how the war had put an end to these friendships. The two of them left as soon as I had finished eating, but came again the next night. This time they stayed longer and we talked about music, books and girls. It was amusing to watch his companion suddenly gyrating about the cell with one hand above his head as he hummed a modern English tune.

The next day I was packed off to Stalag IXc at Bad Sulza, under escort. We arrived late in the day, and I was immediately hustled into the camp prison and locked in without seeing any of my fellow prisoners. My punishment for escaping, I was told, was to be two weeks solitary confinement. This meant two days out of every three on bread and water, sleeping on a wooden bench without any blankets. On the third day I would have a bowl of soup and two potatoes as well as bread and water, and at night I would be given two blankets to cover me.

The cell was tiny, some eight feet long by five feet wide, the window covered with frosted glass and heavily barred. By midday the rays from the sun heated the cell to a temperature that I found intolerable. There were flies everywhere, copulating madly, and they drove me to distraction as they buzzed about the cell or pitched on my face or hands. I was not allowed to sit or lie on the bed during daylight hours, and to make sure that I did not do so the guards would frequently tiptoe to the cell door and peep in through the spyhole.

At night a tin was placed in the corner of the cell for me to use if it was necessary. I would take it out when the guard took me to the washroom each morning to clean myself, then back to the cell where I paced up and down for hours, two paces each way, sometimes three if I shortened my stride. Night-time always came as a relief, for the cell cooled down, the flies settled on the walls and I was allowed to lie down on my bed.

One day I heard a voice calling to me from outside the cell window. I answered and was given instructions to go to the lavatory. Inside I would find a small hole in the wall. If I put my hand into it I would find cigarettes and chocolate. Shouting my thanks, I turned round to see the eye of the guard peering at me through the spyhole. He had heard the shouting, and had come to investigate the reason.

The eye disappeared, and I paced up and down letting time pass before asking to go out, in the hope that the guard would not link the shouting with the request to go to the lavatory. On the ledge were biscuits, chocolates, cigarettes and a book. I hid the booty in different parts of my clothing, pushing the book down an inside leg of my trousers so that it half lodged inside a flying boot.

The guard, instead of locking me inside my cell, called another guard, and between them they discovered everything I had hidden on my person, except the book. The guards were delighted with themselves, for now they had extra rations and they had caught me out.

When they had gone I pulled out the book. It was a trashy cheap novel, but it would while away the late evenings when the guards had settled down for the night. Searching for a hiding-place for it, I found a nail hammered into the underside of the bed. Tied round the nail was a length of string, long enough to wind round the book and hook back onto the nail. It was an excellent hiding-place, for though I was searched every day as well as the cell, they did not find the book. When I left the cell at the end of my sentence I left it there for the next occupant to read.

Though I was bitterly disappointed at being caught it was pleasant to be with the boys again. I spent the next few days building up my strength. My companions were pleased to see me again and we talked late into the night. They told me that after I had jumped from the train some of the others had distracted the guard on duty at the door while one of them slipped into the toilet, replaced the fanlight and screwed it down. It was not until they arrived at the camp and the Germans checked the numbers that they had found one missing. The boys had enjoyed the moment.

The camp inmates were a mixture of our party of RAF prisoners and British Army wounded. We joined forces happily, and daily routines were well organized. Then, late one afternoon, I went to cook a meal for myself out of the contents of a Red Cross parcel. The kitchen, a large one, contained a coal-brick stove. It was alight, hot enough for me to cook on. I had the place to myself and, borrowing a frying pan, I opened a tin of Spam, cut it into slices, then with margarine as fat the Spam was soon frying and crisping nicely. As I bent to turn over the pieces of Spam a voice behind me demanded the use of the stove. I turned to find a huge burly fellow beside me wearing the uniform of an RAF navigator. Politely I told him that I would soon be finished. He insisted that he wanted it now, and began to poke at the fire; dust from the ashes rose in the air and settled on my food. As I pushed him away, he pushed back, and I fell against the stove, burning my arm as I tried to steady myself. The aggressive attitude of my companion and the pain from the burn galvanized me into action, and I hit him with some power with my left hand.

The fighting over the next twenty minutes was hectic, uncompromising, and at times brutal. Within minutes every inhabitant in the camp was close at hand, shouting and cheering vociferously. He was a bull of a man, and at close quarters his superior strength put me in all sorts of difficulty. Time and again he would get my head into an armlock that threatened to strangle me, and in my desperate attempts to free myself we crashed against the walls, into people and against the stove. The frying pan was soon knocked off the stove, the contents flying to the corners of the kitchen. By keeping him at a distance, hitting him with scything blows to the stomach, I finally weakened him, then a left and a right to the jaw sent him on his back, where he was chanted out by the crowd, followed by a cheer that echoed through the camp. There was no doubt in my mind that if I had been the loser the same cheer would have been heard.

The next morning when I appeared on the parade ground for roll-call, I was greeted again with a mighty cheer. The Germans were upset. This latest incident was enough to confirm them in their view that I was trouble. At mid-morning I was ordered to collect my belongings together, and within fifteen minutes I had left the camp under escort and was on my way to the local railway station.

4

Kommando 1547

It took two days travel by train to reach the new camp. To my astonishment the first stop was Saalfeld. We changed trains and soon were winding our way through the very hills I had so desperately wanted to reach while running from my captors. On to Würzburg, and there again we changed trains. This time we journeyed on a single track line, pushing deeper into the hills, until we stopped at a wayside halt, and I was ordered out. High above us sprawled a village and beside it a huge granite quarry.

As the train chugged away up the valley, my escort led the way across the track and up a steep incline leading to the village. Asking directions from one of the villagers, we arrived at a squat, ugly stone building, fronting onto an unkempt area of rough ground; I noticed that its two front windows were heavily barred. Close by stood a small house. Outside its door two soldiers waited as we climbed the slope towards them. One of them was a plump, round-faced corporal with a cunning expression; the other, a private, was tall and thin and looked an unhappy man.

My escort handed some papers to the corporal. I was taken into the house, made to strip, searched thoroughly, then given a French uniform to put on. I protested strongly about my RAF uniform being taken away from me, but in vain. The clothes I was given did not fit very well, and the trousers were very baggy. The corporal also issued me with a pair of socks and a shirt. I was thankful for the shirt, for my pyjama jacket was in shreds.

My kitting-out completed, I was escorted to the building with the barred windows, and locked in. There was nobody around, and I wandered about the rooms to make myself acquainted with my new residence. There were five small rooms, divided three and two by a tiny entrance hall. There was sleeping accommodation for twenty men, ten double bunks spaced out among the rooms. In each section was placed a small stove for heating the rooms and for cooking. On the walls and shelves were photographs and the bric-à-brac of men who had lived in the place for a long while. The bunk allocated to me by the corporal was a bottom one in the section which had three rooms.

It was evening when I heard the sound of marching feet. The door was unbarred, and in they stomped, big men in army uniform, covered from head to foot by a film of quarry dust. The leader, a huge thick-set man, with fierce ginger hair and a voice that made the stones ring, asked me in a broad Scots accent who the hell I was. He stood with his feet apart and his hands on his hips, a giant of a man. I had a mental picture of him at the Battle of Bannockburn, kilted, with a claymore in his hand. They were all Scotsmen, and all on the big side. The moment I spoke, the word "Sassenach" echoed from mouth to mouth.

Despite the fact that I was an Englishman they made me welcome. As soldiers of the 51st Highland Division they had been captured at Dunkirk in 1940, while holding back the Germans to allow other divisions their escape across the channel. They were hungry for news from Britain and I had an eager audience night after night. Their morale was low, and it was good to see how my optimism about the future of the war gave them strength.

The morning after my arrival we were up before dawn, formed up in lines, and marched off under escort to the quarry. Once there we split up, the others automatically moving to the task they had had the day before. I was placed with a group of civilian workers, given a large sledge-hammer, and told to break up a pile of enormous stones that lay nearby. Within moments I had scattered the group to other parts of the quarry as I wielded the hammer with all the enthusiasm I could muster. Splinters of rock ricocheted in all directions, but the stones just did not break. Quickly exhausted by my efforts, and discouraged by the lack of progress I had made, I decided that such a task was beyond me. Though I was given advice, and abuse, about the methods to use, I continued to hit the stones in such a manner that they scattered again and again.

The hammer was taken away from me and I was promoted to the job of shovelling earth and fragments of rock into a tip-up bogey, which, when I had filled it, I had to push to the end of a tip, and send the contents cascading down the slope. The time I took to do this task did not satisfy them, and I was relegated to the position of doing odd jobs about the quarry.

During this time at the quarry, escape was constantly in my mind. I wanted to escape before the winter set in, but they were watching me carefully. It was necessary to hoard up my rations, and to make some kind of map that would help me locate exactly where I was. To add to my problems, I could not persuade the corporal to give me back my uniform. As well as getting back my own clothes I needed additional garments to disguise myself as a workman, for I intended to move by day as well as night when I made my escape.

Winter came early up in the mountains. We awoke one morning in November to find the ground thickly covered with snow, and until the next April the snow remained. All that winter we worked under the most appalling conditions. The temperature plunged to below freezing-point, while the cold, biting winds blasted their way through the hills, driving the snow before them. We would spend hours clearing the snow in the quarry, only to find stones and earth frozen so strongly together that the impact of a pick-axe made little impression. At times it was so cold, that I would just stand with my back to the wind, and freeze where I stood, unable to find the strength or the will to move or to exercise my stiffening limbs. The quality of the food was poor, and there was little of it, and the inadequate clothing and the primitive conditions in which we lived made our lives intolerable.

The guards took their pick of the contents of our Red Cross parcels before passing them over to us. Complaints only led to tougher measures and no redress. Each night we took off our boots soddened by the snow, hung our wet socks to dry by the stove, and set to rubbing some life into our numbed feet. My socks soon disintegrated, and I wrapped pieces of cloth round my feet instead.

The meagre rations of coal or wood for the stoves on which we cooked an evening meal, and dried off our wet clothes, lasted only for two or three hours each evening. Morning after morning we woke to find our top blankets stiff as a battleboard* and covered in white from hoar frost. Our hair and eyebrows too were covered by this frost. My companions rising from the bunks in the dark hours of the morning appeared more like wraiths than real men.

One day at the quarry my boots, soaked by the snow, froze in the intense cold and that evening, when I took

---

*Battleboard is a term used for a Norwegian stock fish which was processed or dehydrated, and sent to P.O.W. camps as part of the diet. It was the length of a cricket bat and perhaps slightly wider. In this processed state it was so tough and rigid that it made an excellent substitute for a cricket bat.

off the wet rags that enclosed my feet, I saw that two of my toes were discoloured. All that night I was kept awake by the painful throbbing of my foot, and the next morning the toes were an ugly sight. The corporal examined them, and told me that I had frostbite and would have to see a doctor, along with one of the Scotsmen who also had frostbitten feet. We were locked in while the remaining prisoners were escorted to the quarry. The two of us clambered back into our bunks to await the arrival of the doctor. My foot continued to throb and I hoped that it would not be long before he came.

The corporal's assistant appeared. His face looked even sadder than usual, as he pulled us out of our beds and shouted at us to get dressed. It was an agonizing business, pulling the cold damp boots over my feet. When we were ready, the guard slung his rifle on his shoulder and gave the order to march. We hobbled out into the snow and set off along the road to Würzburg, hopping and stumbling mile after mile, driven on remorselessly by the guard, who made it quite clear that he did not enjoy the task of escorting us in such dreadful conditions. For seven long excruciating miles we marched, crippled by the pain in our feet.

In Würzburg the doctor covered the toes with a black ointment, wrapped them in bandages, and sent us back. We crawled the seven miles back to camp, cursing the Germans and their ancestors with every step we took. For a week we were allowed to stay indoors, but at the end of the seven days the corporal came in in a towering rage and booted us out of our beds and off to the quarry.

Sandy, the huge Scot, leader of the prisoners, had the job of boring holes in the granite face, putting in charges of dynamite and setting them off, an arduous and often dangerous job. More often than not he had to be lowered down the face of the quarry on a rope tied to an iron stake at the top. I would watch him, sometimes nearly two hundred feet above me, his feet braced against the rock as he drilled a hole in the granite with a cumbersome drill which had been lowered down to him.

The bad winter, poor rations and the constant thieving from the parcels prompted Sandy to take action, not only for himself but for all of us. At the quarry one morning he told the foreman that he would not work any more, until he was given a guarantee that we would be provided with extra rations. The foreman argued with him, then sent for the guards. They came at the double, rifles in their hands. Civilians and prisoners alike gathered around in a semi-circle to watch as Sandy stood, his back against the wall of a hut, waiting to see what would happen. The corporal began by ordering him to start work at once, shouting his words at Sandy with his face only inches away. He had an interested audience and he made good use of his histrionic powers. Sandy remained unmoved, repeating his demands for extra rations. The guards fixed their bayonets on to their rifles, and prodded them at his stomach. Sandy did not flinch, just went on asking for more rations. At this the corporal stepped back, slammed open the bolt of his rifle, and rammed a bullet into the breech. With finger on the trigger, his voice screaming with rage, he ordered Sandy to start work at once, or he would shoot him. I was convinced that he would.

The huge Scot, to everybody's astonishment, drew himself up, thrust his head down into the corporal's face, and in good clear German, that could be heard all over the quarry, told him to shoot and be damned. Indeed, he said, he hoped the corporal would shoot him, for there would have to be an inquiry as to the reason for the shooting. In which case, Sandy went on, they would find out that not only had the corporal been keeping back the prisoners' rations, but also stealing from Red Cross parcels. He was quite sure that the corporal would be shot himself, or sent to the Russian Front.

The next few minutes were pure joy to us. The corporal backed away shouting and screaming. He threw his arms and his rifle in the air. He stamped his feet again and again. He slavered at the lips. Sandy stood, hands on hips, looking at him, arrogant and contemptuous.

The screaming and the yelling stopped. The corporal stood silent, trembling, saliva flecking his chin, totally demoralized. We got our extra rations—and Sandy went back to work.

Night-time, back in our quarters, before we went to bed, and the stove was burning brightly enough to give us the heat we needed, was often for me a moving experience. The men would gather together in one of the rooms, and Sandy, a drum-major in the Black Watch, would turn a tin basin upside down, and with a fork in each hand would begin a roll of the drums. Angus, a piper in the Argyll and Sutherland Highlanders, would join in on a small box accordion he possessed. The tunes were Scottish, sad melancholy tunes that spirited the men back to the Highlands and home. Quietly they began to sing, one I remember well being "The songs my Mother used to sing". The first time I heard them sing, tears rolled down my cheeks and I felt an overwhelming sadness, almost despair, envelop me. Just as dramatically the piper would break into a jig and one of the Scots would jump on to the floor and dance to the wild accompaniment of yells and screeches. Their songs haunted me. Lying in bed, hours later my mind would drift away to England, where I would wander on the downs, a gentle breeze cool on my skin, while above in the blue sky white clouds moved slowly along the horizon. Somebody in the room sang softly to himself, and the longing to be free tore at me agonizingly.

One rare day when the Germans had given themselves a holiday and we were free to move about the hut and the compound, Sandy asked me to help him bring in the food from the kitchen. I followed him down the path to a separate outbuilding. Inside was a buxom blonde *Frau*, busy boiling potatoes in a vat. Sandy talked to her while I watched and listened.

She asked who I was, making comments about my youth and my red hair. Sandy, enjoying the cross-chat, started to invent stories about my exploits. A simple-minded peasant woman, she believed everything that he told her. Pleased with her reactions to his story-telling, he went on to say that because of my youth I had no hairs on my chest, but that a large battleship had been tattooed across it. She demanded to see it. I was embarrassed and did not know what to do. Sandy made no move. Curious and impatient, she ripped open my shirt. There were no hairs on my chest, neither was there a battleship tattooed across it. She turned to Sandy inquiringly, whereupon he informed her that it had been sunk. I laughed and received a mighty clout on the ear. Next moment she had a ladle in her hand, and I was ducking and running for the door!

The winter passed slowly and painfully, but as spring came nearer and the climate softened, the desire to escape began to obsess me again. For all the deprivations we had suffered, I was young and strong. I had learned to cope with the cold and snow, and my body had been toughened by the work in the quarry. Soon the snow would be gone and I had to make my plans for getting away. I knew that I would miss the companionship of the men I had worked with through the winter months, their songs and their bawdy humour. I had gained a lot from their fierce independence and pride.

5

The Second Escape

In preparation for escape I collected together some used hacksaw blades and an old file without a handle. These I carried back to my quarters and hid inside my palliasse. For disguise, I stole from the workmen's hut a battered soft hat and a torn waterproof jacket and hid them under a pile of stones in the quarry. From one of my companions I bought a haversack in exchange for cigarettes. In this I stored the food, chocolate, biscuits and cigarettes I had been saving for the time when I could make my escape. As well as all these activities I had been asking questions about the layout of the countryside we were living in. I knew now that the main autobahn to Munich lay some twenty-five miles to the south.

Everything was more or less ready for the journey, but I still had to get away without being noticed. It was possible to escape from the quarry, but I would be missed within minutes of leaving. To make a successful escape I needed time, and besides I had still to persuade the corporal to give me back my uniform. To be caught by the Germans in a pair of baggy pants was too much of a humiliation. More seriously, their khaki colour and poor fit would attract unwelcome attention.

Easter was upon us, and the Germans took a long weekend for their holidays including Good Friday and Easter Monday. That meant I had four days in which to carry out my plans successfully.

In the room in which I slept, the barred window at the front faced out towards the house in which the guards lived and slept. There was a small square window at the back of the room looking out onto a chicken run. The window was sealed by a framework of three vertical and three horizontal bars welded together, with the horizontal bars bent in at the end at right-angles and embedded in concrete in the wall. With four days with nothing else to do it would not be too difficult to cut through the bars in time.

There was one other problem to overcome. Each night the guard came in, collected our trousers, counted them and took them away with him. Sometimes he just took them away, and I presumed that he counted them outside. I could only hope that the night I chose to escape he would not bother to count them; if he did I would have to pretend that I had forgotten to put them out.

My companions were unsettled by my decision to escape. They had grown into a routine and one or two were worried about repercussions. Nobody tried to dissuade me; two, in fact, decided to help in sawing the bars. One of us sawed away, another stood by the front window to give the alarm if a guard should be seen coming towards the hut, and the other one rested.

The plan was to cut through the horizontal bars down the right-hand side of the window, and push the frame outwards as though pushing open a window. It was hard work sawing, for the blades were blunt, and though we wrapped rags round our hands the blades cut and blistered our fingers. The noise we made as we sawed away was horrifyingly loud but the guards could not hear it from the front of the building.

By the third day my companions' enthusiasm had evaporated and I was left to get on with it on my own. Two cuts had been made and I was now working away at the last. For concealment, after each bout of sawing I would seal the cuts with a cocoa mix which dried out the same colour as the rusted bars.

It was on the third day, while I was making the final cut, that one of the guards walked round the back of the hut. It took him a moment to find where the noise came from. In that split second I whipped away the blade, clamped my hand over the tell-tale cut and bawled out a tune that I hoped the guard would think was a continuation of the noise that had attracted his attention.

The sight of my desperate-looking face peering through the bars, my jaws opening and shutting, while I bawled louder than ever, confused him. He stood watching me as I sang, then deciding that I must be crazy, he tapped his temple, shook his head and walked away. Jumping down from my perch I raced to the front window. He was moving back to the house still shaking his head. Without wasting any more time I sawed away at the bar until the final cut was made, coated it with cocoa mixture and hid the files in my palliasse.

My next task was to rip my trousers in such a way that it would be impossible to mend them. I went to see the corporal and complained about their state and asked if I could wear my uniform, at least for the time being. He agreed, and went off and got them. I returned to my quarters in high spirits confident that all my difficulties had now been resolved.

I warned my two companions that I would be leaving that night. They agreed to help me push out the bars and to see me off the premises, but both had decided that they would not escape with me. We arranged that I should make my departure at eleven o'clock. I informed the others of my plans and arranged with them that they put all their trousers together so that the guard would not have to pick them up from each bunk.

Before the guard came in we were all in bed, tense and waiting. I hid my trousers underneath the top blanket, praying that he would not miss them. He was surprised to find us in our beds but collected the trousers and left, bolting the doors behind him. For the next few minutes nobody breathed or moved as they strained their ears for the sound of returning footsteps. Nothing happened. I relaxed, warm and happy that the first hurdle had been overcome.

At eleven o'clock I slipped out of bed, dressed and collected my haversack. My two helpers crept into the room and we set about the task of pushing out the bars. For all our efforts, the iron frame moved outwards only two inches and would not budge a fraction more. We strained and sweated and grunted but with no success. My companions gave up and went back to bed. Feverishly, I sawed away at the other side of the bars but even as I started I knew that it was a waste of time. I would not finish the job before morning. The noise of the saw on the bars was deafening in the still night air.

Taking out the old file from my palliasse, I reversed it so that I could use the sharp bevelled point as a tool to pick away at the concrete in which the bars were embedded. For hours I worked steadily, digging away, my hands bleeding and sore from the rough edges of the file. The concrete flaked away bit by bit. I felt sorry for those who were lying in their beds close by me. It must have been a nightmare to listen to the noise I was making. It was surprising that the guards had not heard it. Not that it mattered, for if they did not find out tonight they would find out the next morning. I continued picking away.

With a rending crash the frame fell away into the chicken run below. Upset by the noise the chickens squawked madly. The time by my watch was exactly three o'clock. I waited quietly by my bed for a few minutes, but the guards were sleeping well that night. My two friends tiptoed in. A few whispered words of goodbye, and I slipped through the window, to land on the frame below. Again the chickens squawked angrily.

The Second Escape

Hitching my haversack on my shoulders I made for the quarry, where I collected my hat and jacket. Then with an airy wave in the direction of the camp, I clambered out of the quarry and set off southwards in search of the autobahn.

The countryside was snow-covered, the sky clear and filled with stars. It was an exhilarating moment. I was free: and I appreciated my freedom much more now than I had during my previous escape. Even if I was caught again no one could take away these precious moments from me.

Keeping away from the roadside below me, I strode along a winding track, that seemed to follow the valley through the mountains. I had been walking at a fast pace for about two hours, when suddenly my legs seemed to turn to rubber. The hours of concentration and tension spent in getting out of my prison quarters had finally caught up with me. I had to rest. Moving off the track I scooped away the snow from under some bushes, lay down and fell asleep instantly.

Just as suddenly I awoke, my limbs stiff from the cold that had permeated my body. It was a foolish thing to fall asleep in the snow, but all was well, and as I moved away off the track, I soon warmed up.

It was a glorious day: the sky was clear and blue. The sun as it rose higher warmed the air and melted the snow so that the earth showed green and pleasant. I walked on hour after hour, keeping away from the roads and skirting the villages.

Just after midday I stopped to rest in a wood. There was no one to disturb me. I made up a meal for myself, finishing with a piece of chocolate. Lying back in the grass, my hands behind my head I gazed up at the sky happy and contented, till my eyes closed and I fell asleep. When I woke two young deer were quietly feeding just a few feet away. Not wanting to frighten them I lay still, marvelling at such a sight.

During the afternoon, despite all my precautions, I came upon people going about their work; or when occasionally I passed an isolated house, the inhabitants would be standing around in the sun. Many of them were curious at seeing a stranger passing by and some made attempts to speak to me. I forestalled them by smartly raising my arm and saying *"Heil Hitler"*. By the time they had recovered from such a greeting I was well on my way.

It was evening when I came to the autobahn. In the twilight, couples old and young were walking out. I followed them along a path that led down to the roadside, where they stood in groups, watching the traffic roaring past. At the first opportunity I darted across the autobahn and ran deep into a wood on the other side. Hidden away from prying eyes I waited until it was dark.

At dusk, I crept back to the roadside. There was nobody around as I moved out onto the road. In such hilly countryside it would not be long before the road would climb upwards and I would be able to choose my spot and jump up onto a lorry as it lumbered by. Sure and confident, I cast away all caution and strode along the road, my feet clattering on the hard surface. The autobahn bridged over a valley and with only the slightest hesitation I marched on.

From a few feet away, a voice rang out of the darkness commanding me to halt. Anger and dismay at being caught so easily caused me to hesitate. I wondered whether to make a run for it, but already it was too late. The voice materialized into a German policeman and a gun prodded into my stomach.

With the gun in my back, my hands raised, I was marched off to the nearby village police station. It contained a cell, but my captor was so delighted to have me as a prisoner that he could not bear to shut me away.

He wanted to talk, to ask questions, to have a story that he could tell to others. For my part, I did not relish spending the night in a cell brooding on my misfortune. It was a bitter blow which I had brought on myself by over-confidence and carelessness. I gave him my parole not to escape, and we sat comfortably in armchairs, talking and arguing through the night. I ate his eggs and sandwiches and drank the coffee he made, and he smoked my cigarettes and nibbled at the chocolate I offered him. It helped a little to take the sting out of my capture. By morning I was resigned to the thought of being back in camp.

Morning brought two men in soft-brimmed hats and mackintoshes, who took fingerprints, asked questions and left. The policeman whispered that they were Gestapo. The following day two soldiers arrived as escort. It was an honour to be given two escorts.

Our destination was Weiden, a large town north of Nuremberg. We travelled by train. It was not a long journey, and soon I was marching through the streets of the town. Close to the outskirts we came to a large French P.O.W. camp.

My reception was remarkable. As we marched through the main gates we were surrounded by hundreds of Frenchmen, shouting and cheering and jostling the guards so that it was impossible to move. A German sergeant with a number of guards to help him forced a way through the crowd. They hustled me away to a small compound within the camp, in the middle of which stood a brand new 'cooler'. The sergeant informed me that I was to be the first occupant, and pushed me into one of the cells. Inside, there was no furniture of any sort and the place smelt of paint and concrete. After five minutes of leaning against the cell wall I peered through the peephole, and tried the handle of the cell door. To my astonishment the door was unlocked! There was nobody about, and I walked down the corridor and out of the cooler into the small compound.

Behind the barbed wire that cut the cooler off from the rest of the camp a large crowd of Frenchmen had congregated. A great cheer echoed round the camp as I appeared. Cigarettes and chocolate rained down on me while the crowd cheered and cheered. I was astonished at the reception but I enjoyed every moment of it as I waved back.

The sergeant reappeared with his company of guards, accompanied by three French doctors. He was furious that I had got out of the cell, and I was soon back inside. The cell was full of people, and within moments a fierce argument broke out between the sergeant and the doctors. Blankets were thrown down on the floor and when another Frenchman appeared in the doorway with a bulging sack on his shoulders one of the doctors snatched it from him and emptied the contents. Biscuits, chocolates, sweetmeats, bread and cigarettes poured out in a large heap on the floor. There were enough provisions there to last me for a month.

The arguing continued. One of the doctors detached himself from the group and knelt down to lay out the blankets. He pulled my arm and beckoned me to kneel down beside him. I must have looked very bewildered by all the activity going on within the cell for he winked at me reassuringly, and quietly, without wasting words, urged me to eat as much as I could during the night. After enquiring whether I had a watch, he insisted that I be very sick at exactly nine o'clock the next morning. If necessary I was to ram my fingers down my throat and to moan and groan loudly. I was to leave the rest to them.

Suddenly the room emptied, the door locked and I was left to make a bed for myself out of the heap of blankets. I jumped into the middle of them fully dressed, picked out a packet of cigarettes from the mound beside me, took out one and lit it. Too excited to eat, I lay back wondering what was going to happen next.

I woke up the next morning and panicked immediately, for my watch showed that it was already a few minutes past nine. Jumping out of the blankets and making for a corner by the door, I thrust my fingers down my throat and tried to force myself to be sick. My attempts were useless, for I felt fit and rested and had not eaten a single piece of food during the night. At the same time I was worried that I was already too late. Tears poured down my cheeks as I pushed my fingers more violently into the back of my throat. I groaned louder and louder, and in case anybody was watching through the peep-hole I would clasp both hands to my stomach and reel around the cell doubled up. Interrupted in the middle of these antics by an urgent voice calling at me outside the cell window, I stopped for a moment to answer the call. The next moment a shower of cigarettes cascaded through the bars onto the heap and I thanked and cursed my benefactor all in the same breath.

Once again I jabbed at my throat which by now was beginning to feel sore, and burst out into a series of groans that echoed round the cell walls. The door opened and in came the sergeant. I doubled up in front of him my hands pulling at my stomach. This action as well as the sight of my tear-stained face, convulsed by the constant jabbing of my fingers in my mouth, convinced him that something was wrong with me.

Within minutes I found myself in a long whitewashed room full of white-coated doctors, French and German, with their orderlies. I could only recognize the face of the doctor who had told me what to do the evening before. He came close beside me the moment I entered the room.

A German doctor, speaking passable English,

ordered me to strip off my clothes, and thrust a thermometer under my arm. He was immediately called to the other end of the room. My French ally whipped the thermometer away and heated it at a nearby stove. Its reading must have been too high for he shook his head and waved the instrument in the air. Satisfied with the second reading he placed it back under my arm and called the German doctor back. The German examined it, told me that I had a temperature, and ordered me to lie on a bench; whereupon he pummelled me about the stomach and the groin, turned me over and plunged a large hypodermic needle in my bottom.

Off to the hospital ward close by, where I was given a bath and clean pair of pyjamas, and taken to a small single room and put to bed. To my pleasure the bed had springs and for the first time for nearly a year I was lying between sheets. I snuggled down into the bed. It was worth attempting to escape if my punishment was as luxurious as this.

My doctor friend came in to see me, delighted with himself and with the success of his stratagem. When the German orderly came in, as he did from time to time, I was to look sick and feverish; my food I must leave uneaten under the bed. For the rest of the day I dozed happily, woken only by the periodic visits of the orderly and by the arrival of bowls of food at lunchtime and teatime. I shoved them under the bed and went back to sleep.

The sound of closing shutters, and of doors being locked and bolted, awoke me. It was night and I felt hungry. A few minutes later and the familiar face of the doctor appeared in the doorway. He held a dressing-gown in his hand. I put it on and followed him down a long corridor and into a large room thronged with French officers. As I entered, every one came to attention. I was introduced as an English RAF prisoner of war, and the officers clapped.

The Second Escape

It was a heartwarming and good for my morale. So was the sight of tables covered with white linen, and so too the elegant display of plates and silver, wine glasses and at intervals bottles of wine.

The situation had a dream-like quality about it. The food was excellent, the wine delicious and there were cigars to follow. The talk, the laughter and the excitement made it a night I shall always remember.

It was explained to me that I was the first Englishman the Frenchmen had met since France had fallen and they had been transported to Germany. They were happy that England had continued the fight. The Battle of Britain was a great victory, and gave them hope that Germany might be defeated. The party went on into the small hours of the night, and at the end of it I was escorted back to my room slightly drunk but very happy.

For the next few days this was to be the pattern of events, and I looked forward to the evenings with anticipation. Meanwhile, under my bed, the bowls of untouched German food grew in number.

I was surprised one morning by a visit from a senior German officer. A general from the German forces had expressed a wish to see me, and it had been arranged that he should come to the hospital the next day. He impressed on me that I should follow the correct procedure in addressing him, and finally he insisted that I practise standing to attention in bed. This exercise was not a successful one for at his shouted command my efforts to come to attention completely disarranged the bedclothes. I was made to repeat the exercise a number of times, each time with the same result. Harassed and worried, and certain that I was playing him up, his voice grew loud and threatening: any action of mine that upset the general would have serious consequences for me. And with that he stamped out of the room. For the rest of the day there was a lot of coming and going.

The room was cleaned and dusted, though nobody looked under the bed. I was given a bath, clean sheets and clean pyjamas.

The Frenchmen were curious and excited by the general's visit, plying me with questions as to the reason, not really believing that I did not know. Whatever reason he had for coming, I was enjoying the notoriety and attention from friend and foe alike.

The following morning I washed and prepared myself for the meeting. I was anxious only that he might cancel the visit, in which case for everyone concerned it would be an awful anticlimax. Various orderlies, doctors and officers popped in and out, making sure that I was still in bed, and moving pieces of furniture from one place to another. I hoped the general would not look under the bed.

I had advance warning of his arrival. Faintly, at first, then louder, came the sounds of commands, the crashing of army boots at the salute, and the ever increasing noise of marching feet. The door burst open and the room filled to overflowing with officers of all ranks. At the shout of "*Achtung!*" I brought my legs together as stiff as ramrods, hastily re-arranged the bedclothes, and stretched my arms at full-length by my sides.

The room was silent and still, everybody standing stiff and erect. The general entered. He was a large grim-looking man, dressed in field-coat and cap, and decorated with as much braid as a general would be expected to wear. I felt nervous as he stopped at the bedside and looked down at me for some time without speaking.

Without taking his eyes from me he spoke to the senior officer. It was with some difficulty that I followed what he was saying. Why was I in hospital, and why was an Englishman in a French camp? The rest of the conversation was incomprehensible. Then, a slight gesture, and an interpreter crashed to attention by the

The Second Escape

bedside. The general spoke directly to me and the interpreter translated.

I was asked if I was a pilot in the RAF—Yes. Did I fly on bombing raids? Yes. What kind of aeroplane had I flown? I replied that I was unable to answer that question. There was a pause. Then he enquired if I had ever bombed Berlin—I told him many times. (I had bombed Berlin on one occasion, and had been frightened nearly to death by the intensity of the ack-ack barrage, particularly when we had been caught in the searchlights). Having thus embarked on a policy of exaggeration, I had no hesitation, in answer to further questions about the size of the bombs I had dropped, and the success of the bombing missions I had flown, in continuing to exaggerate, carried away for the moment by the excitement of the occasion. I assured the general that reconnaissance and photography had provided ample confirmation of the success of the raids. The general looked pale and angry but stayed well in control of himself. After a few more questions about bomber tactics and losses that I was unable to answer, he left abruptly: and within moments the room was empty, leaving me alone to ponder on the reasons for the visit.

I had not long to wait. The German doctor returned to examine me, and take my temperature. He looked suspiciously cheerful, and I was beginning to dislike him. Having carried out his examinations with the same smug smile, he told me that I was a stupid young man who talked too much. That it would have been better for me if I had kept my mouth shut when being questioned by the general. It appeared that a few nights previously the RAF had bombed Berlin. A bomb had fallen on the general's house and killed his family.

Soldiers entered my room early the next morning, hauled me out of bed by my feet, and as soon as I had dressed, escorted me to the delouser. The German doctor was there, his smile even broader. At his command I took a cold shower, then a further examination. The man was unable to resist the temptation to get at me: life for me was going to be unpleasant. I had caused them a lot of inconvenience by my escapades, not to mention my unfortunate remarks to the general. When Germany had won the war, people like me would get their desserts. Pretty lurid, by his account. I laughed at him; retorted that he must be simple to think that Germany could win. Angry now, he advanced a series of 'facts' that would convince me why Germany would win. Spain: the Spaniards were already fighting for Germany, and it was only a matter of time before Spain declared war on England. I agreed with him that Spain would declare war—but against Germany. When he protested I told him my information came from an unimpeachable source. He was eager to know where I had got this information, but I fended him off, saying that I would be foolish to reveal my source.

Dressed once more in my uniform, and wearing a glengarry given me as a present by one of the Frenchmen, I was escorted out of the camp by two guards, one in front, one behind. As we marched through Weiden I was given a hero's farewell by the innumerable Frenchmen that thronged the streets. One after the other, as I passed by, they stepped out from the crowds on the pavement, came to attention and saluted. To return it was the least I could do, and I responded with enthusiasm. The guards muttered to each other, then shouted at me, but I ignored them. It was good for morale to know that the French had such strong feelings for the British.

My escorts marched me to the civil gaol in Weiden where, after being searched and having my haversack taken away from me, I was thrust into a cell. It was large, and so dark that I could not see the walls. A grill, high up, threw a tiny square of light across the cell.

Slight sounds and movements in the dark told me

The Second Escape

that others beside myself were incarcerated in that lonely dark prison, but although I spent a week in that cell I never spoke to them, nor they to me. During all that time they were sinister shadows in a place of darkness.

I received food each day, and blankets each night. Whatever food the others were given it was clearly not enough, for whenever the soup and potatoes were handed in to me to eat, the shadows moved in from the edges of the cell and hands thrust themselves out of the darkness. I gave away my food, for it was safer to do so. Each night I was given blankets to sleep in on the cold cell floor. I found it prudent to let my shadowy friends snatch them away. It was only when I had left that cell for good that I found out that they were criminals who had been there for a long time, and were destined to remain there.

It was a relief to be ordered out of the cell, put under escort, and marched off through the streets back to the French camp. This time I was put in a small room under guard. For some time I was left alone, to speculate on the reason for being brought back. Finally, an officer appeared and I was marched into a long room, occupied by a dozen officers seated behind a semicircular arrangement of tables. I was made to stand to attention facing them.

A senior officer, at the head of the table, solemnly informed me that I had been brought from the prison to face a court of inquiry, convened for the purpose of discovering the truth of my statements about the entry of Spain on the side of the Allies. I realized at once that I was in a position fraught with danger. It was evident that the doctor had persuaded his superiors that I possessed secret knowledge of Spain's intentions to enter the war, and that they had taken his report seriously.

Somehow I had to convince the court that I had no

secret information. But if they believed me, then the court would be seen to look ridiculous; if they did not, I would have the Gestapo to deal with. At that moment whatever conclusion they came to I would be lucky to escape lightly.

My only chance of salvation lay in showing to the court how stupid and irresponsible the doctor was, and how grossly he had exaggerated the words I had used in our heated discussion on the outcome of the war.

The questioning began. I protested at once at being brought before the court on such flimsy evidence as the doctor had put before them. In response to questions I pointed out that a sergeant-pilot could have no opportunity of obtaining such secret information. They certainly had a complete dossier of my activities as a prisoner of war, none of which could possibly lead them to suspect that I was any more than a pilot in the Royal Air Force. The accusations made by the doctor about me were only put forward to focus attention on himself and make him important. If I was in possession of information as important as they suggested, would I blurt it out under a shower to such a simpleton as the doctor.

The questions pounded out. Again and again I insisted that I had no access to secret information, that I had never been to Spain and that I had no connection with any member of the Spanish Government. Exhausted and angry, the court at last ceased its interrogation. The only officer who seemed to have any understanding of my predicament was the chairman. He spoke fluent English, and had acted as interpreter throughout the proceedings.

I was escorted back to the waiting-room, where I stayed long enough to ponder on my own stupidity, and on the various alternatives the court might decide on as punishment for wasting their time; for I was convinced that I had succeeded in making them understand that I

The Second Escape

was just an ordinary RAF prisoner of war.

Back in the court again, I stood to attention while the chairman spoke of my irresponsibility in making the statements that had caused the court to be convened. He warned me of the serious consequences of any further action, and felt that the court had every right to punish me for what I had already done. He felt however that there had been a distortion of the facts, and the court would take no action. I knew instinctively that it was his influence that had determined the court's decision.

On being asked if I had anything further to say, I complained of my treatment as a P.O.W. in the civil gaol, and asked for permission to be allowed regular exercise each day and to be allowed to smoke. The chairman told me sternly that I should be thankful to be returned to gaol without any additional punishment, and I was dismissed.

Back in my cell, I sat on the floor, thankful that I was in no worse a situation than before. My relief shortly became astonishment when the cell door opened and the guard called me out, handed me my haversack and allowed me to take out a packet of cigarettes and light one of them; he cheerfully accepted another for himself. I was turned loose in the courtyard, to walk for a while in the fresh air and the sun. I walked up and down for a full hour before being escorted back to my cell.

The next day they moved me to another cell, a lighter one, occupied by French prisoners who had attempted escape or had been caught stealing from the Germans: pleasant companions, who taught me the art of smuggling cigarettes and other commodities into the cell under the noses of the guards, an art I put into practice whenever I was allowed out to exercise and to smoke. Their skill and ingenuity in playing up to the guards, and of using them in order to live comfortably in their cell amazed me. We were never short of food and cigarettes, and the days passed rapidly in their company. I lost count of time altogether, but it must have been three weeks or more before the order came for me to get ready to leave.

Once again I had two guards to escort me to the station. The one in charge was abnormally tall and very thin. By contrast his companion was short and tubby. They had never done escort duty before, and from what they said to each other I understood that they had been warned to watch me closely.

Throughout my preparation they fussed and clucked, and pushed me and each other about the place. We stepped out into the street and set off—only to stop, as the guard had decided to fix bayonets, just in case.

A busy road was much too dangerous a place to perform such manoeuvres. I was pushed onto the pavement, the little guard was ordered to stand at my left-hand side, and the tall one then scurried round and positioned himself at my right side. Already a small crowd of inquisitive people had gathered around us.

The manoeuvre was executed with fine precision. The tall guard snapped out a command and they both came to attention. At the next command, they unshouldered their rifles and stood them with the butts resting on the ground. Came another order, and each brought his hand down to his belt and grasped his bayonet; and as a climax to all these actions they whipped out their bayonets and fastened them onto the muzzles of their rifles: that is, the tall guard did, standing smartly erect ready for the next series of commands. The short one had taken out his bayonet all right, but could not fix it onto the rifle. His face grew red as he struggled, still at attention, to join rifle and bayonet together. I looked down at his rifle and gave him a nudge, then pointed to the cap fixed over the muzzle to prevent the barrel from getting dirty. He had forgotten to take it off. He gave me a grateful look; but the tall guard dug me in the ribs with his rifle, to remind me that while he might have a fool as a companion escort, he would not want me to have any wrong ideas about himself.

We set off line abreast, but there were too many people in the way. After another halt and discussion, it was decided that we should walk in Indian file in the gutter, the little one first, then me, then the tall one. Once again the Frenchmen did me the honour of stepping forward and saluting me as I marched past.

At the station I was handed over to the guards who were to escort me to the camp at Bad Sulza. I had hoped to meet all my companions again, but by now they had been transferred to Stalag Luft 3 at Sagan, south of Berlin; all except one, Ray Chown, who had been too ill to move with them but was now recuperating. Within hours of my arrival I collapsed with fever and was taken into the hospital ward. I had acute appendicitis but there were no facilities for operating. All that night I lay in a high fever, my body contorted with pain. Men took it in turns to hold me down while others applied bags of ice to the spot. For a while it was touch and go, but by morning my temperature had dropped and the pain disappeared. For a week I lay in hospital, while the doctor kept a watchful eye on my progress, until at last he felt I was fit enough to be discharged.

6

Stalag Luft 3—Sagan

Fit again, I was on the move once more. This time our destination was Sagan—Stalag Luft 3. Chown too, had now recovered and the two of us, accompanied by our escort of two guards, took the train to Berlin. The journey was long but not tedious. We travelled on passenger trains, always in a compartment that had been reserved for us. Passengers passing along the corridor would stop and peer curiously at us until waved away by one of the guards.

We stopped at many stations *en route*; and at the larger stations where we would remain at the platform for ten minutes or more, one of the guards would slip away and return with mugs of tea. We shared our sandwiches and cigarettes. After a while, however, the journey began to take on the proportions of a nightmare. While the train waited at the platform, we would watch people moving about the station or talking to each other, while we ate our food, or smoked and chatted among ourselves. It was all so much an informal matter-of-fact daily routine of travelling from one place to the other, that I felt at the next stop I would get off the train and go home. Only the rifles leaning against the wall of the carriage were a reminder of the reality of war, and the fact that soon I would be isolated again from this everyday world; surrounded by wire, and by guards with guns who would not hesitate to shoot, if, in a moment of confused thought, I tried to step back into that world.

The camp at Sagan, built in a clearing in the midst of pine trees, looked like a fortress: high double fences of barbed wire, with rolls of barbed wire festooned between them; watch-towers around the perimeter, manned by men and machine guns; mounted on frames beside them, powerful searchlights waiting for the night when they would spring alight, their beams searching the compound for any erring prisoner bold enough to step outside his hut. Around the perimeter guards, rifles slung on their shoulders, moved back and forth.

Inside the compound stood a series of long low huts, raised two to three feet above the ground on stilts so that the guards could see beneath. Seismographs were buried at intervals along the perimeter wire, so that any attempt to tunnel a way out of the camp would be recorded in the form of vibrations by these instruments. The Germans rightly felt that they had built an escape-proof camp, but to make doubly sure that no prisoner would prove them wrong, they had built up a team of highly trained men, distinguished by the overalls they always wore, who moved around the inside of the compounds and through or under the huts day and night, looking for any signs of escape activities. At night alsatian dogs were let loose in the compound. Lying there awake, we could hear them sniffing at the ground beneath the huts.

So confident were the Germans that they had built an impregnable fortress, that they brought together old 'lags' like Wing-Commander Day, who had already escaped several times. These men had been in captivity for a long time and were well-versed not only in the techniques of physically escaping, but in the forged passports, identity cards, up-to-date train passes, and the business of persuading guards to bring in cameras, film, paper and pens, various tools and other equipment, by a gentle form of blackmailing them or bribing them.

Stalag Luft 3 was later made famous by the exciting and original escape of three men, as told in the story of *The Wooden Horse*, all three succeeding in getting back to England; and the tragic episode in which seventy officers escaped by tunnelling only to be recaptured, followed by the murder of fifty of these officers, all shot in the back.

My hopes of seeing my companions again after so many months were rudely dashed when I was thrown into the 'cooler' to serve another two weeks of solitary confinement for my escape from Kommando 1547. The door clanged behind me, the key rattled in the lock and I stood in the middle of the cell looking at the eye peeping through the spyhole in the door.

The cell was square and small and built of concrete with a tiny barred window high up in the wall, furnished with the usual wooden trestle which was my bed. A pipe, which ran along the wall close to the floor, disappearing through the walls on either side, was the only other object of interest. I decided that it was used as a form of central heating in the winter months, and felt that the Germans must be getting soft.

The diet was the usual plain bread and water, and there were no blankets, but as I was now becoming an experienced old lag, I had no difficulty in accommodating myself to the routine. The days dragged by, as I paced backwards and forwards, concentrating my mind on those wonderful moments of freedom when I had the world to myself.

One day when, tired of the pacing, I took a chance and sat down against the wall, I found I could hear a sound of tapping on the pipe. It was very faint, and at first I could not locate where it came from. It came again. Checking that nobody was at the spyhole I knelt down by the pipe and tapped on it with my fingers. Immediately came an answering tap. Faintly, through the wall, I heard a voice but I could not make out what the unknown person was saying. I examined the wall where the pipe disappeared into it. The cement round the joint had contracted and there was a slight gap between the pipe and the wall.

Putting my lips to the crack I called quietly, asking who was there. Then placing my ear in the place of my lips, I listened. Faintly but clearly, I heard a voice asking me to identify myself. This I did, and the voice then took on a tone of urgency. The speaker told me that he was a Squadron Leader Bushell. He had escaped into Czechoslovakia and joined up with a group of partisans. They were caught, and the Gestapo had interrogated him, accusing him of sabotage and demanding that he be executed. He had been sent to Stalag Luft 3, and placed in a cell until a decision could be reached between the Gestapo and the Luftwaffe as to whose prisoner he was. Bushell went on to say that he had been unable to make any form of contact with anybody else, and was afraid that he would be taken away again and shot.

The sound of the guard outside the cell door brought me swiftly to my feet, but he was not interested in my activities and his footsteps died away. I knelt down by the pipe and asked Bushell what he wanted me to do. He replied by asking me how much longer I would be in gaol, and when I told him I thought it would be another two days, he asked me to see the senior British officer, tell him of our conversation, and ask him to get in touch with the Swiss Red Cross immediately and demand his release before it was too late.

Promising Bushell that I would do what he asked, I wished him luck and we said goodbye. Two days later, as soon as I was released and entered the non-commissioned officers' compound, I asked to see the camp leader and stressed that the matter was of the utmost urgency.

Stalag Luft 3—Sagan

Dixie Dean, Warrant Officer, aircrew, was the camp leader. I told him Bushell's story, and said that in my opinion Bushell was in great danger. Dean promised me that he would see the senior British officer that day, and would do everything to make sure that Bushell would be released. I was impressed by Dean's stature and authority.

Bushell was released from the jail and put into the officers' compound. The sequel, however, was tragic. He was involved in the success of the 'Great Escape' and was one of the prisoners to get out of the tunnel and make his escape, only to be caught and handed over to the Gestapo—who made sure that he would not get away from them again by shooting him in cold blood.

A bunk was found for me in one of the huts, and I teamed up with a group of prisoners. We pooled the contents of our Red Cross parcels, and took turns in cooking, washing up and all the jobs like carrying water, digging our small sandy patch of garden, and other sundry tasks. I joined a football team, and exercised daily by walking round and round the compound.

Getting vegetables to grow in the sand was a thankless task. Watering was not enough. We collected a variety of seeds, and planted them eagerly enough, but nothing ever grew. We felt that the Red Cross should have sent parcels of earth with the seeds.

Despite my name, I was no gardener. Our gardening expert, an agricultural type, put forward an idea that he thought would resolve the difficulties of growing vegetables in sand. He produced a couple of large empty tins with handles on them, and tied a long length of string to each handle. We were to go in turn to the latrines, lower the tins into the pit below through the hole in the wooden seat of the lavatory and bring back the contents in the tin to the garden. We protested that the idea was disgusting, and that apart from the odour the vegetables would be tainted, and even if they were not, how could we eat them knowing by what method they were grown?

Patiently he explained that when the Germans cleaned out our cesspits they sprayed the contents on the crops, and that the potatoes and *Sauerkraut* that were given us as a part of our weekly diet had been forced up by this process. As he wanted a quick growing garden, the method he would use would be more concentrated! Taking us outside to the patch, he persuaded us to dig a series of deep trenches, and sent us off in relays to fill the tins from the pit, and empty the contents into the trenches. He then covered it with a thick layer of sand, sprinkled in the seeds, and covered them with a thin layer of sand.

To our delight, beautiful fresh green lettuces sprouted before our eyes, and tomatoes grew and ripened into luscious fruit. For a short season we ate well, our garden the envy of other prisoners.

Retribution came when the cesspit cart, heavily laden, rolled past our window on its return journey out of the camp. It was an old-fashioned model, cylinder-shaped, and drawn by a horse. The wheels of the cart were wooden and pegged in by wedges. On this particular occasion, as it drew level with the window, one of the wheels fell off. As the cart began to lurch in our direction another wheel came off. The container hit the ground and we watched silently as the liquid contents flowed over our garden to lap against the wall. Even as we watched the remaining wheels spreadeagled sideways, and the container rolled slowly over, releasing the remainder of its contents in the form of a small tidal wave.

Slowly it dawned on us that this was not a simple accident. For reasons we would never understand, somebody had knocked out the wedges and made off with them without the Germans knowing. If we had ever caught him we would have buried him in our garden!

A young prisoner named Grimson had his bunk just

across the room from us. He was a slim quiet person who spoke German fluently. Every day he was to be seen talking with one of the overalled guards, always the same guard. The two would stand by an open window talking animatedly to each other. We came to the conclusion that Grimson was intent on brushing up his German.

One day Grimson was missing. He had escaped. The method he used was a brilliantly conceived idea and well executed. The first time he had met the guard, he saw that they were of the same build and height, and that there was a certain resemblance in their features. His knowledge of German made it simple for him to strike up a friendship with the guard. They stood by the window because the guard was nervous in case he was caught gossiping with a prisoner. This suited Grimson, for he could study every facial movement, every mannerism and gesture when the guard spoke. For weeks Grimson prompted him to talk about his family, his home and his hobbies, and as the friendship grew, he asked him what he did when he was off-duty, what his plans were for next week, and when he was going on leave. Meanwhile the Escape Committee was busy forging documents that would get Grimson through the gates of the compound and out of the camp, as well as further identity documents to help him travel freely once he was away from the camp. Grimson grew a moustache similar to the one the guard possessed. He often stood by the gates when he knew he was entering or leaving, making notes of the pattern of entrances and exits.

Then the guard told him that he was going on leave the next day and told him when he would be coming back. This was the time Grimson chose to make his escape. It was a triumph of artistry and good ground work. Nobody challenged him as he made his way through gate after gate, until finally he stood outside the camp, a free man.

Late one evening, long after the prisoners had been locked into their huts, my appendix began to give me discomfort. As the night wore on the pain became acute. Once again I was held down firmly while cold compresses were applied to my stomach to try to alleviate the pain. Others banged on the door and shouted to attract attention but nobody came. When morning came, the Germans were alerted, and I was rushed off to a hospital not far from the camp. Within minutes I had been given a spinal injection, and was being operated on by a French Negro doctor. After completing the operation, he told me I was a lucky man. I was delirious for two to three days.

Eight days after the operation, though not yet fully recovered, I was returned to camp. My weight had fallen considerably, and I was forced to move about very carefully. Dysentery spread through the camp and I fell victim to it. Weak as I already was I had little resistance to offer and grew steadily weaker.

Desperately looking for a cure I came upon a tin of kaolin. Emptying the contents into a mug and filling the mug with water, I stirred the mixture thoroughly and drank it down. Results were almost immediate, and though I suffered agonizing pains I was cured. With the help of a few extra rations authorized by a British medical officer, I built up my strength once more.

News came through that a number of RAF prisoners of war were to be transferred to Stalag Luft 1 at Barth, a camp close to the Baltic Sea, not far from Stralsund. The Germans asked for volunteers and I gladly stepped forward. I welcomed the opportunity of getting away from Sagan, for it offered no hope for the future. Perhaps it was the pine trees that surrounded and shut in the camp. They stood clustered together, as though awaiting a signal to fall upon us and devour us. I was suffering from claustrophobia.

7

Barth

The volunteers for Stalag Luft 1 assembled in the compound. The roll was called and the party marched off to the railway station at Sagan, escorted by armed guards. From there they embarked on a special train to Barth, arriving at night after a quiet, uneventful journey.

Next morning after roll-call I wandered around the compound, taking stock of our new camp. I estimated that there were two hundred prisoners who had volunteered to come here, and my first impressions were that we had made the right choice.

The first thing I noticed, with relief, was the absence of pine trees. Barth was built on a peninsula. Through a thin screen of trees some distance away I caught a glimpse of water. The air was fresh, with a slight tang of the sea. Half a mile away to the north stood an army barracks, where men were trained to handle and fire ack-ack guns.

The camp itself was composed of three compounds, all surrounded by high barbed-wire fences. The prisoners occupied one of them, the Germans guarding us another, and the third was a large field which we were allowed to use at prescribed times to play football or rugby. The huts were partitioned off into a number of small rooms each holding six prisoners. Through the huts ran a central passage with the rooms opening up on either side.

Life at Barth was relatively pleasant and undemanding. We had a regular supply of food parcels, the German food was plentiful and well cooked, clothes and blankets were easy to obtain and our parcels of clothes and tobacco as well as letters, all from home, came regularly into the camp.

The Commandant was a decent man. He had been a prisoner of war in England during the First World War. As such he had been treated well, and in turn he looked after us. The Security Officer too, had spent several years in England, and spoke excellent English with a good upper-class accent. A clever man, with an understanding of the English mentality, he made escaping such a difficult proposition that we had to resort to tunnelling as about the only means of getting free.

We had only just settled in, when he put on a demonstration of what might happen to a prisoner if he should succeed in getting through the wire. A German guard appeared, heavily padded around the arms and legs. He represented an escaping prisoner; and at a given signal he set off across the open fields, cheered on by the watching prisoners. He was not allowed to get far, before two alsatian dogs were unleashed. To yells of encouragement from us all, the dogs streaked towards the victim who, padded as he was, stumbled his way across the field, looking back again and again with an anguished look on his face as the menacing animals closed in on him. Out of breath, he tripped and fell and the dogs were upon him. Growling ferociously, one grabbed his arm and the other a leg as they had been trained to do, pulling him in different directions until it seemed an arm or a leg must part company from his body.

The dog-handlers, following up, snapped the leashes on the animals and pulled them away. We clapped the victim heartily as he limped past the wire, back to his quarters. I wondered how many times he would wake up from a nightmare of hounds homing in on him to tear him limb from limb. Despite our cheering and clapping, it was a sobering thought that one of us might be the next victim, and without any padding to save us.

Exercising on the football field was one way of getting rid of our frustrations, and we made good use of the field whenever we were given the chance to play on it. Almost every afternoon we would flood into the field, each taking part in various forms of physical activity for a couple of hours.

One afternoon we had just settled into a routine of recreational activities on the playing field, when we were distracted by the sight of a column of soldiers from the army barracks, approaching along the road which ran adjacent to the field. Everybody stopped to watch as they marched resolutely with much stamping of feet. As they came closer, the officer leading them gave a command and they burst into song. The first one they sang, I recognized as "We march against England". I could not help admiring the smartness of their drill and the way they kept in step. Their voices were strong and they sang well.

The column was split into a number of groups each led by an N.C.O., with a gap of some yards between each formation. The officer-in-charge led from the front. When they finished a song, the officer would give an order, by numbers, followed by *"eins, zwei, drei"*, and still in step they would begin to bellow out another marching song.

When the soldiers appeared along the road three days running, we began to get the impression that their route alongside the camp was not just an accident, but a propaganda exercise. We felt the commandant of the barracks wanted to impress on us how strong and disciplined was the might of the German Army as personified by his soldiers.

Impressed though we were, we would gather in a large group by the wire whenever they appeared, their heads held high, and we would clap and cheer or else a group of P.O.W.s would emulate them, marching parallel to them in ragged step, bursting into discordant song at the command of a falsetto *"eins, zwei, drei"*.

The Germans began to get embarrassed. Things came to a head when one of the prisoners, a fluent German speaker, identified the manner in which the orders to sing were given. After a few rehearsals with some of his friends, he stood by the wire one day, with them around him. He waited until the column was half-way past and had come to the end of a verse. Then, in perfect imitation of the officer leading them, and above the clapping and cheering, he gave the command, followed by *"eins, zwei, drei"*, but on the wrong marching foot. The soldiers obeyed the command automatically, resulting in the sight of soldier after soldier changing step in a series of hops and skips, while at the same time trying to sing in time and step with the others who were also hopping and skipping.

Neither the officer nor his men understood the reason for the breaking up of the disciplined marching of the column. It was like music to our ears to hear the abuse he screamed at the unfortunate men! When the break-up occurred for the third time in the same place, the officer knew the reason why. There was a row between the two commandants, and we were asked not to do it again.

Attempts to escape were rare, and all resulted in failure. Whenever this happened we were shepherded onto the playing field and identified one by one, until the Germans were satisfied they had accounted for everyone. It was a long, cold, miserable affair. On the first occasion this happened, when my turn came to be identified by the Security Officer, he looked at some papers in front of him, shook his head disapprovingly and told me that because of my escapades, my name was now in their 'black book'. He warned me that I was considered to be a 'dangerous' prisoner, to be kept under observation.

Months later, another attempt to escape was foiled. We were again herded onto the playing field and identified. The check over, the guards opened the gates into our own compound and the prisoners streamed through. Those in the lead noticed at once that the Germans had failed to place their men back in the watch-towers. An astonishing sight ensued; dozens of prisoners scrambling up over the barbed-wire fences, dropping to the ground and haring away over the fields.

The alarm was given immediately, and grim-faced guards surrounded the compound, their guns at their shoulders, while others set off to recapture the escapers. The rest of us were sent back into the field to be checked once again. It was night by the time, cold, bored and hungry, we were allowed back into our quarters. Sadly, all the escapers were caught, each of them spending two weeks in the cooler before rejoining us.

Along with others I spent many of my days at Stalag Luft 1 digging tunnels in an attempt to escape. The odds were heavily against us, for the Germans were aware that a successful tunnelling operation would mean a mass exodus of prisoners, which if timed properly, would enable most of them to be well away from the camp before the Germans found out. As at Stalag Luft 3, the huts were raised on stilts so that men and dogs could check if the ground had been disturbed by any digging, and seismographs were planted deep in the ground to record any vibrations caused by digging. Whenever the Germans became aware that a tunnel was being constructed, they planted men outside the compound who watched with powerful binoculars for any unusual patterns of movement.

One tunnel that we dug came close to succeeding. That we got so near without the Germans discovering it, was through using another old tunnel we had dug earlier in the year and then abandoned. The Germans did not bother to fill it in, and forgot about it. We started the new tunnel at the entrance to the old one, and so joining them together we were able to empty the soil from the new one into the workings of the old, instead of throwing it on the surface, wet and glistening for the Germans to find. When we sealed up the tunnel at the end of a shift, our trapdoor into the shaft was three feet under the soil.

To get outside the wire, the tunnel needed to be forty to fifty feet long. The soil was fairly firm and we did not use any props to bolster the roof. We were taking a chance, for if there was a subsidence while we were working at the face it would have been extremely difficult to get out. We could only move forwards or backwards on our stomach, with the roof inches above our heads. To wriggle backwards along the length of that tunnel when one was in difficulties gave one no opportunity for speed, only a feeling of panic.

Day by day we took it in turns at the tunnel face, cutting away the soil with knife and tin, and pushing the loose soil under our bodies and behind us. The next man in the tunnel would scrape it together and pile it into a cardboard box, which he would then drag back to the shaft.

To get air, we would at intervals along the tunnel bore a hole in the roof with a rod, until it broke through to the surface three to four feet above. It was fascinating to be watching and waiting for the rod to appear like magic from the earth, waggling like an inebriated worm that had lost its sense of direction. The sighting of the rod gave us an indication of our progress towards the wire, and by lining up the holes we were able to make sure that we were keeping in a straight line.

This elementary form of giving air to the perspiring digger and his mate was, however, unable to deal with the need for a light at the face. The best method of providing the light we wanted was by filling a small round tin with margarine into which we inserted a wick made from a piece of pyjama cord. But the lamp, while giving light, consumed the air in the tunnel, so that the digger could only work for a few minutes at a time, before he needed to rest and gulp in air, before attacking the face once more.

We had reached a point twenty feet from the entrance, and I was at work digging at the face, when I found the way barred by a large pipe running at right angles to the tunnel. It was too dangerous to dig over the top of the pipe, for the tunnel would be close to the surface, and the roof would cave in if somebody walked over it. I therefore began digging underneath, and had reached a position where I was stretched half one side, half the other, my body bent like a bow. As I dug away, a feeling of giddiness overcame me. I was passing out! There was a leak in the pipe and the air was tainted by a disgusting smell. For the first time I felt frightened and trapped. For a few moments I panicked, only to wedge myself firmly under the pipe.

Reason came to my rescue. Moving gradually and carefully, I freed myself, and wormed my way backwards until I came to an airhole. I drank greedily the air that blew down it. Later, we sealed off the leakage, and widened the tunnel under the pipe, continuing to make steady progress. After weeks of digging we estimated that it had reached the wire. Two more days and we should be far enough outside the compound to dig upwards and make our escape.

That night we discussed our next move. We knew that the Germans were aware that a tunnel was in the making. In spite of the constant searches by the guards, we were close to breaking out, and the excitement was intense. Some of us were for closing it down for the time being in the hope that we would lull the Germans into believing we had abandoned the tunnel. Others argued that the Germans must realize how far we had dug, and would not stop searching until they found it. The vote was in favour of continuing.

The next day we went back to digging. Twice we were forced to abandon work, as the guards were seen moving into the compound. The second time we closed up the tunnel, for there were too many Germans around.

The following day we re-opened the shaft, only to close it up quickly when the rumour reached us that a large contingent of guards were expected in the compound. Our informant thought that they had discovered the whereabouts of the tunnel, and were waiting for us to start work before raiding the compound, so as to catch us red-handed.

Miserably, we dressed and dispersed. I stood by a window from which the main gate into the German compound was visible. The whole camp had been alerted to the fact that something was about to happen. All faces were turned towards the gate, everybody still and waiting.

For twenty minutes nothing happened; then, suddenly, there was a movement close to the gates. We waited. The gates opened, and in raced three closed vans, normally used for deliveries of food to the kitchen. They skidded to a halt, doors opened and guards, rifles in hand, tumbled from the vans and spread out, surrounding the hut in which I was standing.

The Security Officer, with his pistol held high, leapt from the leading van and rushed in through the door, followed by half-a-dozen guards. I stepped out into the passage and leaned against the wall, watching to see what would happen next. With a crashing of boots on the floor they came into sight. As he reached me the Security Officer paused, recognizing me, then with a puzzled look, dived into the room I had just vacated, lifted up the trapdoor in the floor, and sent his men scuttling through the hole to catch the tunnellers as they came up to the surface.

I stood by the door and watched. By the look on his face, I could tell he knew he was wasting his time but could not understand why his ploy had failed. It was the only time I ever saw him really angry. His men re-appeared through the trapdoor, their faces and clothes coated with sand and earth, to tell him what he knew already. He cleared the huts, while the prisoners cheered his cloak-and-dagger methods.

More guards appeared in the compound with spades and picks, and dug away the ground until gradually the whole length of the tunnel was revealed. The prisoners were kept at a distance while the digging was going on. To my surprise, the Security Officer called my name and ordered me over to the site of the tunnel. The Germans had uncovered it carefully and were taking photographs. I looked down into a neatly constructed tunnel, that lead from underneath the hut in a straight line to a position underneath the wire fence. Though still upset, I felt pleasure at the fine piece of tunnelling we had done with the crude tools that we possessed.

I saw the pipe which had caused me to panic, straddling the tunnel. The Security Officer pointed out a huge rock balanced delicately above the trench, admonishing me for taking such risks and putting other people's lives in danger. What could we have done, he said, if the rock had fallen into the tunnel while men were working in it?

For some time the English and German Governments had been discussing terms on which prisoners of war could be exchanged. The intermediary had been the Red Cross. An agreement was reached. Men who had lost a limb, or suffered from galloping consumption, or any other disease which had incapacitated them, or were found to be insane, were to be repatriated. A team of medical experts from the Red Cross, accompanied by a panel of German doctors, were visiting prisoner of war camps to examine any prisoner who might be recommended for repatriation. The camp commandant informed us that this team would be visiting Barth.

Some prisoners began at once to work out methods by which they could deceive the medical experts into sending them home. One idea, which met with no success, was to swallow pieces of soap. Under an X-ray the soap would show up as a black spot, which indicated that the prisoner had consumption. Others worked out ways in which they thought, hopefully, that they were disabled, and a few others behaved as though they were insane. Despite all these ploys only one man succeeded.

Jock Kerr was a friendly, optimistic person, and we enjoyed his company and his jokes. Gradually he became silent and morose, and was to be found alone at a distant part of the compound, gazing out through the wire. He gave up all exercise, and at night lay on his bunk reading books on philosophy, as well as others with obscure titles. He began to underline passages in the books he read, and write notes in the margins, leaving the books in all sorts of odd places, with the pages open for all to read.

We became disturbed by this eccentric behaviour and alarmed by the notes he wrote in the margins of books. Eventually the British doctor ordered him into the hospital bay and kept him under observation. Kerr's condition continued to deteriorate. The doctor sent him back into the compound, with strict orders to all prisoners to keep watch on him whatever he did or wherever he went.

Kerr finally committed an act which convinced British and Germans alike that he was insane. On a gloriously sunny day, in full view of the guards in the watch-towers, he climbed the wire fence between the recreation field and the German compound. Everyone stopped and watched, as he clambered laboriously from strand to strand. The guards in the watch-tower stood open-mouthed at the idiocy of the man. Before they could take any action prisoners were running to the base of the tower and shouting at the guards not to shoot, that Kerr was mad and did not know what he was doing. As Kerr slipped down the other side guards rushed in and collared him, dragging him off to the cooler where he was locked in a cell.

When the Repatriation Board came to Barth they examined Kerr, classified him as insane, and recommended that he be sent back to England when the exchange of prisoners took place.

When he left for England he took with him letters to relatives from the prisoners. He was a walking mailbag. I received a letter from him some months later. In it he told me he had visited my mother, and told her how well I was. He also mentioned that he was flying again in the RAF, but was not allowed on operations.

Kerr was a resourceful man and I admired him for his ingenious and clever deception. He was a brave man too: in climbing over the wire fence, he had taken a calculated risk, and a terrifying one. Other men had climbed wire fences in various camps in Germany, and had died violently in a hail of machine-gun fire.

There was a period of hectic activity, when the RAF sent over planes to bomb Rostock and Peenemünde. The nights were filled with the roar of bombers passing overhead. German night-fighters were also in the air above the camp, and we could plainly hear the chatter of machine guns. Simultaneously the army barracks down the road opened up with its ack-ack guns. The prisoners locked in their huts were shouting and cheering the roar of each bomber as it passed overhead. It was pandemonium.

Although the window in our room was shuttered, we could force it open sufficiently to peer out and watch the action going on. The camp was in darkness, and our room was lit only by the explosion of shells and the reflections of the searchlights. All the occupants of the room were straining to look out at the same time. The noise and tension built up as the bombers, returning from their targets, flew low over the camp, the ack-ack batteries firing furiously at them. We hoped that the commandant at the barracks had forgiven us for playing musical chairs with his soldiers and would not use the occasion for dropping one or two shells on the camp!

Another bomber skimmed across the huts, and as we shouted and cheered and jostled each other to see what was going on, a loud 'crack' sounded outside the window. Immediately one of the boys shouted out that he had been shot. There came another 'crack', and we dived for cover underneath the bunks. Unfortunately in the darkness we all seemed to dive for the same bunk. The cracking of heads and the swearing and cursing sounded far worse than the shots we had heard. There was confusion as we sorted out our arms and legs in the darkness. The wounded man continued complaining, and as soon as we had untangled ourselves and were safely under the bunks, somebody asked him where he had been shot. When he said that he had been hit in the backside, we became hysterical. An anxious voice from beneath a palliasse asked if there was any blood, and we howled like hyenas.

The raids petered out, and the lights came on. Hauling out our wounded companion from beneath a bed, we pulled down his trousers to find out what injury he had sustained. On the left cheek was a large bruise, in the centre of which the skin was grazed. Next we examined the wall of the hut, and soon found a hole where the guard outside had fired through the woodwork in anger.

A large number of Russians arrived in the camp, and

were billeted in tents on the recreation field. They were a ragged, emaciated crowd of prisoners, who had survived a march from their homeland into Germany. We were warned not to make contact with them, and were locked in our own compound while they were there.

Rumours were rife about the state of the Russians. The two most horrifying were that there was an outbreak of typhoid among them, and worse, that in their hunger they resorted to cannibalism. What was a fact, is that many of them died while staying at Barth.

We were appalled by their appearance, and tried various ways and means of getting food in to them from our Red Cross parcels. The simplest method was to throw food over the wire to them, but this caused the Russians to fight each other. The guards were hostile to our actions, and we were forced to stop. There was not much else we could do without the co-operation of the guards. Every one of us felt guilty, lining our stomachs with food while they starved on the other side of the wire. It was almost with a sense of relief that we woke one morning to find that they had gone.

During the summer months we would spent the hour before lock-up sitting outside our huts in the cool evening air, talking to each other or walking round the compound. On one of these occasions, our cook, an army man who had changed identities with an RAF prisoner and joined us in the camp, was demonstrating, with the use of a broom, how to carry a rifle on parade. He was a huge, wild-looking fellow with a loud voice. Addressing commands to himself, he would then carry them out, and we were fascinated by the dexterity with which he used the broom when 'sloping arms' or 'fixing bayonets', or when marching and countermarching.

In the middle of this display, the gates of the compound opened, and in came two guards to pack us off into our huts for the night. They were new to the prisoners, and looked an ill-assorted couple, reminding us of Laurel and Hardy. Their approach was hesitant, due to the bawling voice of the cook and the wild look in his eye. From a safe distance they gestured to us to go to our huts, but we were always slow to obey orders, a form of passive resistance that always upset the Germans. This time we made no move at all, for there was the prospect of an interesting confrontation between them and the cook.

Full of enthusiasm, encouraged by an admiring audience, the cook executed an about turn with precision, shouting out his own commands in a voice that could be heard all over the compound. It was at this moment the guards plucked up courage to interrupt him, asking him to stop and go inside the hut.

The cook halted, did a smart right turn to face the guards, fixed a baleful eye on them, and in thundering tones shouted the order to fix bayonets. The guards were apprehensive. At his next command he brought up the handle of the broom in the crook of his arm, so that it was pointing at them. Moving back a step, they looked at each other anxiously. At the command 'charge' he broke into a run, gaining speed with each stride, the word 'charge' drawn out and echoing among the huts, as he thundered down on them. It was too much for them, and they ran for safety. The guards at the gate, as well as those in the watch-towers, were used to the prisoners' strange brand of humour, and were happy to enjoy the discomfort of their comrades. The cook stopped before the gates where his victims had sought sanctuary and went through the actions of bayonet practice before shouldering his 'rifle' and marching back into the hut.

Roll-call was held twice a day, once first thing in the morning, and for the second time in the late afternoon. We would form up in lines and wait for the arrival of the

Security Officer and his men. The camp leader would bring us to attention and the guards would begin the count to make sure that all prisoners were present. It was invariably a long drawn-out affair, for the Germans checked the figures by counting again and again. We agreed among ourselves that they were notoriously bad mathematicians; but the fact was that they were afraid that somebody might have escaped between roll-calls. The figures were checked a number of times. The Security Officer was informed of the numbers, then suddenly we were called to attention and dismissed. In the winter months the cold wind and the snow took toll of the prisoners as they stood on parade. For many of them lumbago and chilblains were a common complaint. In the summertime when the winds were warm and gentle, the prisoners livened up many a roll-call by confusing the counters. We were never surprised when the Germans found on checking numbers that there were more prisoners on parade than they had in their books. When the lads were in a mischievous mood, they would arrange that selected prisoners placed in the middle of the ranks, having been counted, would crouch down and run between the lines to reappear at the end of the columns and be counted again.

One morning on parade the counters found that ten prisoners were missing. The Security Officer was about to send a search party around the compound to find the missing men, when from behind the huts came the sounds of drums and fifes. Into view came the men, led by the army cook. They were dressed as girl guides, with blue skirts barely covering their thighs, army boots on their feet and no socks. One or two had bandages round their heads, another, his arm in a sling, and yet another, one leg doubled up behind him, hobbled along on a crutch. The cook marched with a long pole held high, from which flew a tattered flag. Some played on kettle drums made out of milk tins, while others played on penny whistles. The tune was barely recognizable as "It's a long way to Tipperary". Their short skirts and army boots with hairy legs in between were an indescribable sight.

They marched down the front of the parade, and on passing the Security Officer, who was watching with mouth open, did a smart eyes-right and saluted, then marched on their way. The Security Officer, having counted them as they passed, was satisfied. Poker-faced, he returned the salute and dismissed the parade.

And so the months passed by, until one day we received orders to pack our few belongings, ready to move out of the camp the next day.

As we marched in columns down the road towards the station in Barth, I could not help looking back at the camp that had been our 'home' for so many months. The commandant had been a good man who treated us as human beings. He was a civilized person, quiet and gentle, who accorded us the respect and dignity that made us admire him for his understanding of our circumstances.

8

Heydekrug

Though we were sorry to leave Barth, we were excited and curious about our new destination. The Germans had given us no information about our movements, and rumours spread rapidly that we were returning to Stalag Luft 3 at Sagan. All speculation ceased as we marched into the railway siding adjoining the station, to be replaced by a grim silence as we were confronted with a chain of box-wagons, the sliding doors pulled back to reveal black dirty interiors, each one empty except for a half-section of an empty oil drum positioned close to the opening.

Without wasting time the guards butted us with their rifles, urging us into the wagons, filling up each box until it seemed they could take no more. The hatch swung across, plunging us into darkness, and we heard the clanging of the bar being bolted into place. Inside each box was a mass of men standing, squeezed tightly together holding their breath, their eyes straining for any sound that would help them understand what might be happening next.

For a long while nobody moved or spoke. The tension inside the box-wagon was so strong I could feel my skin prickling; a kind of fear seemed to catch at my throat. This was a new level of relationship between the Germans and ourselves, and because it was unexpected it conjured up dark sinister fears of what was coming.

A long, long silence followed. The new environment,

and the lessening of tension made men want to relieve themselves. We were beginning to accustom ourselves to the semi-darkness and by dint of shuffling around one could reach the oil drum. For a while it was in constant use. The stench of urine and other waste products contaminated the air. A feeling of claustrophobia caused me to break into a sweat and I had to repress an urge to strike out indiscriminately at the people around me.

At last the train clanked into motion, criss-crossing points until it reached the main line. For the next few days, with only the occasional stop, the train rattled along, the wagons swaying to the motion, causing the liquid in the drums to slop from one side to the other. I was thankful not to be positioned next to it as some of my companions were. Men grumbled and cursed as others, changing their stance to ease their aching limbs, inadvertently stepped on toes. The movement of the wagon and the stench in the air caused some to vomit. There was no relief whatever position one took up, and it was not until the second day that, exhausted and stupefied, we no longer felt the pains or cramp in our bodies. We herded closer together, to allow a few men at a time to sit on the floor and sleep.

On the third day of our journey, during one of the halts, we were startled by the sliding back of the door and the appearance in the opening of a guard, revolver in hand. He jumped up into the wagon, and kicking out with his feet cleared a way into the corner. Behind him, in a line outside the wagon, stood others, their rifles pointing at us.

From where I stood I could see little of what took place, but when the guard had left and the door clanged to once more, a hubbub broke out among the prisoners. A prisoner had hidden a file in his clothes, and while the train was in motion had been busy cutting a hole in the wagon floor. The Germans had been thorough, and while inspecting the underside of the wagons had come upon the tell-tale cuts in the floor. The prisoner concerned was lucky not to lose his life.

Late on the fourth day the train stopped. The door slid back and we were ordered out. I half climbed, half fell out of the wagon, my muscles by now hopelessly unco-ordinated. Crouched close to the ground, I could feel the blood coursing painfully through my cramped body, my eyes screwed shut against the blinding light, while the smell of the sweet fresh air filled my lungs. A shout from the guard, and I moved away to join others already forming up into some semblance of a column. Along the line, figures were falling from the wagons one after the other. The guards, impatient and intolerant, shoved us and butted us into lines.

Finally the last man lined up in formation, and we stood, looking worse than animals, our hair matted and grimy, our faces black-lined and filthy, our uniforms crumpled and stained, and the smell from our unwashed bodies polluting the air. The camp commandant, a tall Prussian officer with the rank of major, stood watching us, his face angry and disgusted.

We were marching through pine trees to our new camp. It was a place called Heydekrug, near Königsburg, the capital of East Prussia. It was a large camp separated into four compounds, one for the Germans, one for American aircrew, one for our companions from Stalag Luft 3, and the fourth one our own compound. The other compounds were full, ours was empty and waiting for us.

We were billeted in wooden huts, each consisting of a large room, which was the combined living and sleeping quarters for fifty prisoners. There were two small rooms off the main one, used for the purposes of washing and as toilets. Our bunks were built up in tiers of three, one above the other. Bed boards or slats placed side by side covered each bunk, upon which was laid a straw palliasse. Each man had two blankets and a straw pillow. In the centre of the room stood a stove which heated the room.

Next to the huts was a small field which we quickly marked out as a playing area. An empty hut was converted into a theatre. There were no other amenities.

The moment we entered the compound we made for the huts. Without wasting time we selected our bunks, teamed up with others to share our rations, washed ourselves and our clothes and settled down to our new routine. Many of us had been prisoners of war for a long time. We were professionals, hardened and tempered by the fortunes of war. Our optimism on the outcome of the conflict was balanced against our ability to survive until it ended. We were realistic and rational in our assessment of the situation we were in, eschewing all emotion and exaggeration. Our physical condition was an important survival factor. Each day we walked round the compound for an hour or two, played physical games, and worked daily at exercises. This was necessary, for on the debit side was the lack of sufficient food, the poor quality of it, and the irregular kind of diet we had. For example, *Sauerkraut* was on the menu at least one day each week. This sour cabbage was boiled in water and handed to us in buckets. The smell of it hung over the compound all day, and our stomachs sickened at the thought of eating it.

As well as our diet, the countless hours spent on roll-call sapped our strength. The winter months were bad. Snow lay thick on the ground, and the east wind cut through our inadequate clothing, shrivelling up our bodies as we stamped up and down to keep the blood circulating in our bodies.

Another important factor in the art of survival was the relationship between ourselves and our captors. It had a demoralizing effect on many of the prisoners. We learned the hard fact that we were at the mercy of every

German. They could curse us, kick us, spit on us, and shoot us if necessary. They could rouse us out of our beds at any hour of the night they chose, they could make us stand out in the cold all day, they could search us and all our belongings at will; and when the whim took them, they could deprive us of food. It was our acceptance of the inevitability of such actions, and with it, a remarkable if somewhat strange sense of humour, which helped us to forge the will to survive, and the determination never to show them that they were our masters, even though they held the trump cards.

To have given in, to lie down on one's bunk and die, or to become unbalanced, even mad would have been easy. A number of men did, not because they wanted to, but because the odds stacked against them were too great. For most of us the experiences we underwent gave us a ruthless determination to live, and with it the strength and will to overcome the handicaps that were a part of our daily lives.

We practised the art of passive resistance, prolonging the argument or discussion with gentle words. When forced to move, we did so slowly and deliberately, always knowing how far we could push the situation. To understand the character of the German, and to play on his weaknesses, was a part of our survival kit. When he came to us in triumph to tell us of some major disaster, we would chide him, telling him that it was all lies, or the facts had been exaggerated, that it was just propaganda.

A source of strength to us was our ability to collect the pieces of equipment to make a crystal 'radio', primitive but functional. For years we were able to listen to the BBC news each night. When we were on the march we carried a set with us.

During the long cold winter nights we played bridge or chess. There were card schools for poker and pontoon, the stakes being cigarettes. The alcohol experts were busy developing and making stills. From potatoes, raisins, even ersatz jam, they concocted deadly brews. In our hut we had taken possession of a large barrel. All kinds of fruit and vegetables went into it to make what was to be called the 'classic brew'. We watched over it daily, as it fermented, impressed by the antics of the experts as they checked it, tasted it and took its temperature.

Lady Luck stepped in to make sure that we celebrated in style. A prisoner in the hut caught the mumps, one or two others followed him to the sick bay, and the Germans isolated us until the incubation period was over. We were confined to our hut and nobody was allowed in, not even the guards. There were no roll-calls and we could stay in bed as long as we liked. Our food was dumped each day on the doorstep. One felt sorry for those who had caught the mumps, but blessed them in the same breath for giving us freedom from the normal routine.

The Germans gave us extra food and coal rations, and the stove blazed merrily day and night. We made plans for the binge of all time, the night before our incubation period ended. When the other prisoners were called out for roll-call we would crowd the windows and, like little kids, we would smile or gesture or stick out our tongues as our companions mooched broodily past. At night we sat up late listening to records; one of them that sticks in my mind was "Skylark", sung exquisitely by Dinah Shore.

The binge was a great success. The wine in the barrel having been tested and tasted, was ready for consumption. We drank and sang and told stories far into the night. Men stupefied by their first taste of alcohol since being taken prisoner slept where they sat, their limbs fashioned grotesquely by the loss of co-ordination; others climbed the rafters, where with their feet straddling the beams, they swayed ominously, singing loudly and crudely to the occupants below, while others, more agile, hung by their legs upside down from the rafters, scratching at their armpits and making animal noises.

In the midst of this rowdy rumbustious scene, the door burst open, and a German officer accompanied by guards stormed into the hut. There was a momentary silence, then the singing began again, deliberately, the prisoners watching the officer's face intently. He shouted again and again for us to stop, and when it seemed he had gained control of the situation, another group would start up. It was not until he pulled out a revolver that the noise died away.

Having got his way, he became more reasonable, but insisted that the party should end immediately and that we should return to bed. Unbeknown to him, high above his head, one of the prisoners was imitating him. He swung by his legs and one hand from the rafters, following every gesture made by the officer, adding *"Ja, mein Herr"* to every order given, and saluting with his free hand. A guard watched him, his eyes wide with astonishment and wonder, but he made no move to stop him. The swinging ape overdid it, when he let out an appalling scream that had us all jumping out of our skins with fright. The officer, nearly out of his mind, screamed back at him; collecting himself, he demanded name and number, whereupon the ape came back smartly, informing everybody that his name was Smith and his number was one, two, three, four, five, six. This information the officer wrote slowly in his book. With a further warning to get to bed at once, he wisely retreated. There were many sore heads the next morning, but all ended well and the Germans did not attempt to arrest Smith, one, two, three, four, five, six.

At this time the German Wehrmacht were worried by the increasingly spectacular escapes from RAF prison camps. Many of the prisoners caught escaping were in possession of forged passes and passports, railway warrants and German currency. They realized that the guards in the camps were being corrupted by the prisoners, and were taking bribes in exchange for the use of documents and equipment.

At Heydekrug things came to a head when one of the guards was caught red-handed supplying information to the prisoners. To avoid being tortured into confessing what he had been doing he hanged himself in his cell. Dixie Dean, the camp leader, warned us all to stop trading.

The Gestapo were called in to see what they could do to remedy matters. As part of their overall plan they decided to search the entire camp. Early one morning, we were awakened by the sound of running feet. We jumped from our beds and ran to the window, in time to see hordes of men in civilian dress, followed by the camp guards, running into the compounds. It was estimated that five hundred Gestapo were involved in searching the camp.

Within moments the huts were surrounded. We dressed hurriedly and thoroughly, for we knew that we would have to spend the day outside in the field while they searched the huts. The Gestapo paired off and two of them entered our hut. We were ready and waiting for them.

They were well dressed, as were the others we had seen running into the compounds. Most of them wore three-quarter-length overcoats, hats of some kind, scarves and gloves; some carried walking sticks. They looked well-fed and arrogant, and conducted their search with gusty humour.

We were lined up, and each prisoner was forced to strip. He and his clothes were thoroughly searched, and when that was over he was bundled through the door, where he was taken over by the guards and escorted to a penned-off area on the field. The Gestapo warmed to their job, and had soon discarded their coats and jackets and continued their searching in their shirt-sleeves.

Despite all the care and thoroughness of the Gestapo, the prisoners were able to piece together the crystal set they had brought out with them, and listen to the news. The newscaster's war bulletin was good, boosting our morale, making up for the inconvenience caused us. The guards looked cold and miserable, upset by the vote of no confidence in them, and angry at the arrogance of the Gestapo. The wiser and more experienced guards were more optimistic. They knew that the Gestapo had little knowledge of the handling of prisoners of war, and they preferred to wait and see what happened at the end of the day.

By late afternoon the search was over. The Gestapo invited us into the huts to show us how successful had been their mission. On entering our hut we found the two men, still in their shirt-sleeves, standing by a table near the door. They were hot and perspiring but very satisfied with themselves. On the table stood cardboard containers full of clothes, maps, inks and other suspicious materials. The room had been devastated; blankets, palliasses and clothing littered the floors. It would take us hours to clean up the mess. We were cold, hungry and very angry, but we thanked them for their courtesy, complimented them on their thoroughness. Some stopped to ask them how they had been so successful, while others shook them by the hand and patted them on the back. Each one of us found time to pay them a compliment as we filed past. They seemed overcome with pleasure at our ability to accept defeat so graciously.

It was when the last prisoner had filed past, and they turned to collect the boxes, that they understood the reason for our magnanimity. All the containers were empty, except for pieces of string and bits of debris that the prisoners had put in as a consolation. Worse was to come, for with sudden apprehension they turned on their own coats and jackets, to find that they too had gone, as well as the hats and scarves. They stood dumbfounded, their faces changing colour rapidly while they waited for the earth to swallow them up.

The ranting and shouting began. As they heaped abuse on us and waved their fists in the air, we laughed louder and louder, then cheered and cheered and cheered. They were frightened men, for what they did not know, but which we were certain of, was that the same incidents were going on in all the other huts.

And so it proved. It had been a disastrous day for the Gestapo. They had been humiliated, and in front of the ordinary everyday guards that they despised and thought were incompetent. When they left the hut, we rushed to the door and windows to cheer them on their way. The guards raised their rifles as we appeared, but we knew that it was a token gesture. Gestapo after Gestapo emerged from the huts, without coats and hats, cheered on their way out of the compounds.

A cartoon appeared in the English Press some months later, showing the Gestapo chief, hair standing on end, being addressed by his second-in-command, who stood to attention at the salute, in his shirt-sleeves and without his trousers. Behind him in lines stood a body of men all in various stages of undress. The chief is being told that the mission has been successfully accomplished.

That night, the excitement over, we cleared up the hut, sorting out our belongings and making up our beds. We knew the Gestapo would not forget this outrage, and that sometime in the future we would have to pay a price for what we had done.

News came into the camp that a large number of RAF officers had escaped from Stalag Luft 3 at Sagan. They had successfully completed a remarkable tunnel, devising techniques in tunnelling never used in an escape before. The news gave a marvellous boost to our morale.

When next we heard that fifty of the officers who had escaped had been shot in the back, we did not believe it. The story persisted and the thought that men could perpetrate such senseless cold-blooded killings sickened us. One of the men murdered was Squadron Leader Bushell, the man I had talked to through the cell wall while I was in the cooler at Sagan.

Another order was given by Dixie Dean, telling us to quieten down and not to give the Germans any excuse to take action against us. We behaved like model prisoners, giving offence to nobody; but despite these precautions, the terrible slaughter of those young officers made us uneasy about our own future. One could feel the tension that was building up.

A rumour started that an order had been given to shoot all RAF prisoners of war. Hitler had demanded it, backed by Himmler and Goebbels. The Wehrmacht were opposing the order, saying that there would be dreadful reprisals against German prisoners held by Britain and other countries. The rumour grew, alarmingly reinforced by the sight of German soldiers digging gun-pits round the perimeter of the camp, and installing machine-guns which were directed at the camp and manned day and night by soldiers.

For three weeks we moved cautiously around the compound, eyeing the guns and the men standing beside them. Life in the camp became almost unbearable, so great was the tension. Men talked in whispers and laughter disappeared completely. We were rats in a trap: if the order was carried out there would be no escape from the lethal gunfire.

In this atmosphere of fear, I woke one morning to find armed guards around my bed. I was told to get my things together, and marched out of the hut. I was taken to a small hut in the compound, normally used as a storehouse. As I arrived at the door of the hut, so did another prisoner, also escorted by guards. We were ordered inside, and told that this place was to be our quarters from now on. We would not be allowed outside.

I opened the door and went in followed by my companion. The single room was small and sparsely furnished; there were two bunk beds. Choosing one I sat down and looked at my new room-mate. He was as nervous and worried as I was. As we conversed, it became apparent that we were both troublemakers. We surmised that the Germans had gone through the records of the prisoners and selected us as two persons likely to cause them concern. I was afraid that the Germans might have decided to deal with us as an example to the other prisoners.

The first night in our new quarters gave us an indication of what was in store. We had hardly settled in our beds when the door burst open and the guards rushed in, hauling us out of bed at gun-point. They ransacked the room leaving us to clear up the mess and go back to bed. In the late hours of the night they returned to tear the room apart once more. These sudden visits became a feature of our existence over the next few days and weeks.

Then, early one morning, while all the other prisoners were locked up in their huts and sound asleep, the guards burst in, and once again at gun-point we were ordered out of our beds. But this time it was different. We were forced out of the hut, and marched out of the compound in our pyjamas and bare feet. The fears that I had been trying to conceal from myself, from the moment I had been isolated from the others, came flooding to the surface. I stole a glance at my companion. He was white-faced and grim. He too was thinking the thoughts that were in my mind.

Our escort led us out of the compound, to a low black building, where the two of us were lined up against a wall. The guards stepped back and stood facing us, their rifles at the ready. A German appeared, and photographed each of us in turn. Time passed. The guards stood motionless, their guns never wavering. I felt the damp earth under my feet and the chill spreading up through my legs. The early morning wind was sharp and frosty, cutting through my pyjamas, yet I did not feel cold, nor did I shiver. My mind was a welter of thoughts, all confused; I felt no fear nor any other emotion. We stood as in some old engraving, etched in the clear morning light. That scene is fixed for ever, indelibly, on my mind.

Somebody barked out an order. We marched back in to the compound, back to our hut, back into bed, where I lay motionless, unsleeping, for many hours.

One day the soldiers left. The trenches were filled in, the machine-guns dismantled. Peace on earth in our little place, for a short while. We talked aloud and began to smile, but things were changing. Leaflets were handed out to the prisoners, printed in black and red lettering. We were described as murderers of innocent women and children. In large capitals the leaflet warned us of the consequences of any attempt to escape. The prisoner who had impersonated one of the guards at Sagan borrowed Ray Chown's watch, telling him that he would return it after the war. He never did. Successfully escaping from the camp at Heydekrug, he made his way to the Baltic coast, to be caught in a small town near the sea. They took him into a field close by the town, and shot him in the head.

The news bulletins gave us hope that the war would soon come to an end. The Russians had begun their advance towards Germany, the Allies had landed in

Normandy. We waited each day with impatience to know when it might end.

9

Evacuation

July 1944. The Russian Army was advancing into East Prussia. Our hopes of freedom were rising, mingled with doubts about the intentions of the Germans towards us. In the meantime, daily bulletins from our own 'radio' kept us well informed on the progress of the Russians. We listened for the sounds of gunfire and watched the skies for Russian aircraft. We prayed that the Russians would overrun the camp, but at the same time we were afraid of the consequences. Plans were made in the event of the arrival of the Russians, and plans also were discussed as to what action we should take if the Germans decided to liquidate us rather than let us fall into the Russians' hands.

All plans were shelved when the Germans suddenly gave the order for us to get ready to move at once. We packed hurriedly anything that would be of use to us, using hold-alls, kitbags and haversacks to carry it in. I filled up two small battered suitcases I had acquired and tied them together with a piece of rope, allowing me to sling the rope around my shoulders so that the suitcases hung on either side of me. This gave me the freedom to use my hands when necessary for other purposes.

Along with American prisoners of war from another compound we marched in a long straggling line to the sidings where we climbed into box-wagons. We were crammed into them, the door was pulled across and bolted, and we were on our way without a moment's delay. As usual, there was no room for anybody to sit down.

The wagons rolled into the docks at Memel late the same night. We followed the Americans onto a ship berthed nearby, down iron ladders into the bilges. The hold was already full of bodies by the time I got to the bottom of the ladder. It was a hideous sight to see the hundreds of men, each struggling for a place to sit without being submerged by the others around him. The pressure of others coming down the ladder sent me crawling over the squirming mass of bodies until I found a niche between two ribs of the keel, where I could stand leaning against the ship's side. The hatch was battened down, and in complete darkness we settled in.

The engines clanked to life, the hull shivered and vibrated, and we were moving slowly out to sea. The boat soon began to pitch and roll, and it was only with difficulty that I prevented myself from falling onto the hordes of bodies below me. Men began to vomit from seasickness and I soon joined them. As the boat rolled more violently I clung to the ribs on either side of me, while my mind wandered over the various ways in which the boat could sink, bombed by Russian planes, sunk by a torpedo, or swamped by a gale. We were a bad cargo, and in rhythm with the movement of the ship we rolled to and fro.

From time to time a section of the hatch above us was opened up and a battered old bucket filled with ersatz coffee was lowered to us. In the half-light the scene was worthy of a description of hell. A body rising up here and there only to sink down again, a flurry of arms, and above it all a babel of sound. The foul air from the smell of bodies and the vomit made it hard to breathe. I was violently ill for the whole journey. For two days and nights we sailed and lived in these indescribable con-

Evacuation

ditions, a nightmare that went on and on, with no knowledge of when it would end. The ship docked at Stettin, and immediately the Americans were ordered out leaving us to spend another night in the hold.

Next morning we left the ship. We crossed the quay in the grey morning light and clambered into the wagons waiting open to ship us off to our next destination. This time the Germans had barricaded a small section of each wagon, and into these sections they squeezed twenty-four prisoners. The other two-thirds of the wagon were for the six guards allocated to each group of prisoners. By sitting between each other's legs, all of us facing in the same direction, we could sit, but it only worked for a short while.

The day was beautiful and warm. The sun rose gently in a deep blue sky and the surface of the water rippled and glinted, making small chuckling sounds as it slapped against the quayside. Framed in the opening, a large modern cruiser lay berthed just beyond the boat we had left, a formidable-looking warship bristling with armaments.

Nobody seemed in a hurry to send us on our way. We sat patiently, talking quietly to each other or looking out at the sky and the sea, or watching the seamen on the cruiser moving purposefully about the deck. Our guards lay sprawled in the straw talking and smoking. The warmth, the quietness and the stillness acted like a drug, one by one we fell asleep.

A sound, faint but familiar, reached our ears. Suddenly everybody was awake, tense and still, straining to catch the sound more clearly. The sky framed in the doorway began to change colour, blackening with wave after wave of planes. I glanced at the guards. They had stopped talking, lying still and taut as their senses translated the message to their brains. The volume of sound grew louder, and now the first echelon of planes were near enough for us to recognize them as Flying

Fortresses.

There was no sound from the German defences. The American bombers had caught them by surprise, and were already running up onto their target unmolested.

The sudden wailing of a siren sounded the call for action. On board the cruiser men dashed madly about the deck. The long slim barrels of the guns swung towards the sky. Our guards slithered quickly out of the wagon, leaving us trapped behind the barricade.

The guns on the cruiser opened up, soon joined by flak guns situated round the port. Black blobs of smoke hung in the sky as the shells exploded among the planes. The din from the guns was deafening and, above it all, the throbbing of countless aeroplane engines almost split our eardrums with the intensity of noise. An acrid cloud of grey smoke filled the wagon and crept out over the water, hiding the cruiser under its dirty pall as canister after canister of gas belched out its hideous contents, in an attempt to hide the port installations and shipping from the prying eyes of the bomber crews. Our eyes watered, and we coughed madly for want of air.

Bombs began to fall, screaming and whining as they plummeted earthwards. Trapped in a gas-filled wagon, we buried our heads in our hands as they exploded around us. The wagons lurched and swayed and jumped in the air. Buffeted and bruised, we huddled closer together as salvo after salvo of bombs exploded and erupted with increasing violence. The bombers roared overhead, harried by the hundreds of guns, firing continuously.

It all stopped suddenly, miraculously. The smoke drifted away and the blue sky appeared; we crouched, wiping our streaming eyes, staring at each other disbelievingly. We were still alive. None of the prisoners had been hurt. The cruiser appeared out from the fog, undamaged; the guards struggled back into the wagon, and the hate in their eyes boded ill for our future. But we were alive and the sky had never looked so beautiful.

A short while later, the train pulled jerkily away from the quayside. For three days we travelled in our confined space, taking it in turns to stand so that others could sleep. There was no conversation with the guards. The atmosphere was hostile and we felt a foreboding of things to come.

Early on the morning of 20th July 1944 the train came to a halt in a small country town. The barricades were pulled away and we clambered out. I stretched my aching limbs and breathed in the lovely scent-filled summer air. The countryside was rich and warm. If only I could lie in the long green grass and dream.

I collected my two suitcases and placed them at my feet, then like the others, I stood beside the wagon and waited. Hours passed, and the sun rose high in the sky. One could only guess that we had arrived too early, and that the Germans were not ready for us. I noticed that as time went on the number of guards increased, until I estimated that there were some three hundred of them. There were two distinct groups, one composed of tough, villainous-looking men, the other group made up of young lads, striplings of fourteen to sixteen years of age. The lads were dressed in uniform similar to the other guards, and each one had a rifle slung over his shoulder. The older groups carried a mixture of rifles and sten-guns. It did not take me long to realize that the youngsters belonged to a Hitler Youth unit.

Our camp leader, Vic Clark, moved down the lines of waiting prisoners, stopping to talk quietly now and then. When he reached our group he warned us that something unpleasant was going to take place. He did not know what it was, but asked us to stay calm, keep good discipline, and no matter what the provocation not to panic, but stay together. His words caused us no surprise, only apprehension as to the form of the treatment to be meted out.

An order was given. I slung the rope tied to my suitcases over my shoulders and followed the others out of the siding on to the roadway. We formed up in a column and stood waiting for the next move. For two hours we stood, holding our possessions, while the sun beat down upon us. An alarm signal began to tick inside me as I watched the guards sorting out pairs of prisoners and handcuffing them together. Women began to gather on either side of the column and shouted obscenities at us. Encouraged by the guards they spat at us as well.

I avoided looking at the women, staring down the road that stretched ahead, bordered on either side by trees. The guards sorted themselves out, stretched in a file on either side of the prisoners, the Hitler Youth alternating with the experienced soldiers. As the youngsters clipped bayonets onto their rifles, their smooth round childish faces glowing with excitement, they became more frightening and menacing than anything else we had encountered as prisoners of war.

The noise of dogs barking made me look round. More guards had arrived on the scene, pulled along by savage-looking alsatians straining at their leashes. There were so many guards around our column now that the thought crossed my mind that the Germans expected an attempt to break away and escape into the woods.

We were told to march. Automatically I lifted my foot to step forward as did the others only to find that the column was not moving at all. I was positioned halfway down the column in an outside line of prisoners, and I could not see why we were not moving forward. The only thing to do was to march on the spot. By word of mouth passed down the ranks we were told that the Germans were having a joke. The front ranks were forced to stand still while the others behind were made to march forwards. We closed up tight, while the guards shouted and pushed and jeered.

Then the Germans grew tired of the game, and suddenly we were marching forward. Some of the women ran alongside for a few yards, shouting and spitting, but they were soon left behind, and there was no sound now except the heavy marching of the columns.

A kilometre of road passed under our feet. The rhythm of the march built up. Everybody was in step, tense and expectant. Ahead lay a bend in the road. One of the prisoners dug me in the ribs and nodded at the woods on either side. I looked and saw small groups of soldiers spaced at intervals in the woods on either side, each group manning a machine-gun. The word was already passing down the column, that under no circumstances was anybody to break away from the column.

We marched round this bend, and another, to where the road straightened out ahead as far as the eye could see. At the beginning of the straight a car was parked on the verge, and perched on the running-board stood a slim young-looking officer, immaculately dressed. His creases were perfect, his white jacket spotless, and the angle of his cap set the seal on the image he wanted to present to us. As I passed by I saw a long ugly scar down one side of his face. In his hand he held a revolver.

Deliberately, very slowly, he lifted the gun high in the air and pressed the trigger. The sound of the shot echoed through the trees. This was the moment the Germans had been waiting for. Suddenly, with savage brutality, the guards drove into our ranks, bayoneting, clubbing and kicking. The dogs were unleashed, and encouraged by their masters, leapt at their victims, bringing them crashing to the ground, then tearing at them with their teeth, growling savagely.

Ahead of me a tall Canadian turned his head. The

stock of a rifle hit his skull, and I watched his blood spurt upwards into the air before he fell to the ground. A thick-set heavy-looking guard with an unshaven face, the barrel of his sub-machine gun in his hands, picked me out as his next victim. I ducked as the weapon swooped down on my head, and it hit me between the shoulder blades. I flew forward onto my face on the ground. As I fell, half-stunned, I instinctively threw off the suitcases that encumbered me. I rolled over onto my back in time to see my attacker, arms above his head, in the act of striking me again. The stock splintered the surface of the road as I slithered to one side. Without waiting for the next assault, I leapt to my feet and ran, stumbling over fallen bodies, discarded kitbags and hold-alls. The others were running too, and as I ran and ducked and weaved to avoid any further injury, my eyes took in little isolated scenes from around me.

One of the young boys, his lips drawn back, was thrusting his bayonet again and again into the backside of a limping prisoner. I caught a glimpse of a prisoner manacled to his unconscious partner, trying pitifully to drag him along at the same time kicking out at the dogs that leapt at him. Bill Sykes, a Yorkshire character, chose to run on the outside of the guards. He was unmolested. All the time voices called out in English persuading us to try and escape. I understood the reason for the groups of soldiers in the woods. The Germans wanted an excuse for a massacre, but the discipline of these seasoned prisoners, and the words of the camp leader, denied them the excuse.

For just over two kilometres the bloody chase lasted, before, like a haven of rest, we saw the gates of our new camp ahead of us. The remnants of us who were still standing were made to lie face down, and ordered not to move or speak. Horse-drawn carts were sent to pick up the others, returning to the compound and dumping them on the ground like sacks of potatoes. The Americans were there too, lying face down on the ground, having had the same treatment the day before. They had lain there since, without food or water or any first aid.

Late in the evening the Americans were at last given food and water. Though warned by the Germans that any American seen sharing it with the English would be shot, they did so as much as they could. Such generosity and disregard of the consequences showed us the nobility of an unusual race of men. For the rest of the night we lay motionless under the glare of the camp searchlights. The guards stood alert and watching, their guns at the ready.

Next morning the Americans were called out in groups and before the day was over only the English remained in the compound. Another night passed and it was our turn. I was escorted with others to a long narrow hut. Down one side of the room stood a line of tables and behind each one stood a German. Each one of us was allocated a table.

We were ordered to undress completely and lay our clothes on the table. Standing naked, we watched them examine our clothes minutely. Any unusual document or implement found in our pockets provoked a barrage of questions and occasionally aggression. Stripped and naked though we were, we too were searched. We opened our mouths for them to inspect. They looked through our hair, under our arms, between our legs, our toes and our fingers. This examination of our bodies was interrupted on occasions by a straight arm punch in the face, a kick in the groin, or, when told to bend down, a savage kick in the behind that would send the recipient crashing against the far wall. We then dressed to the accompaniment of further blows.

The search over, we marched out of the hut and into a large compound, where, in groups of ten, we were shown our new quarters. These, 'dog kennels' as we called them, were fourteen to sixteen feet long and six feet wide. To get inside we had to crawl on hands and knees. Once inside it was impossible for anybody to stand upright. To sleep comfortably was impossible because of the cramped conditions.

During the summer months thunderstorms built up around the camp each day, and at night unleashed their fury at the camp. Lightning struck the earth around us, until one night one of the kennels was hit. One man died and the others were burned and shocked. Some of the storms were so violent, we preferred to stand out in the rain, rather than sleep in the kennels.

In keeping with the kennels we lived in, the Germans treated us like dogs. The food for each group of ten men was doled out into one big bowl, no discrimination shown in the mixture. As the Germans would give us no cutlery, we were forced to sit around the bowl and dip our fingers into the mixture, using them like chopsticks in order to carry the food to our mouths.

Meanwhile in a neighbouring compound large wooden huts, more like the ones we had been used to, were being built. The rumour went around that when they were completed they were to be our new homes.

10

Stalag Luft 6—Grosse Tychau

The huts in the other compound were completed at last, and rumour became a fact. We moved into our new quarters. Compared to the dog kennels they were luxury apartments. Each room held sixteen prisoners and was furnished with eight double bunks and a table. A small stove with its ration of briquettes stood by the wall.

Every bunk was lined with bed boards, on which we laid our palliasses. The boards were about four inches wide and in the beginning there were a minimum of twelve to each bed. They were the right size to shore up tunnels, and were also used as firewood when coal was short.

Our rations each day were a tenth of a loaf and a skimping of ersatz margarine. The main dish was usually watery *Sauerkraut*; swedes, cooked and mashed up, were an occasional alternative. Rarely, we had potatoes. Ersatz coffee or mint tea were our staple drinks—both tasted vile.

Red Cross parcels of food arrived and we received one parcel a week each while there were enough; but supplies were erratic, and often we had to go without. As prisoners we had always been hungry, but our hunger now was acute. One man only in our room was allowed to cut the bread and share out the meal each day. A tenth of a loaf allowed for three thin slices for the day. Our man, after smearing on a tiny bit of margarine, would lay out the slices on the table. At times we could not help circling it looking for the piece that was bigger than the rest. The sharing of rations in each room caused more bitterness and resentment than anything else that took place in the camp.

It was difficult now to find the energy to play any form of sport. The pastime of walking round the compound almost disappeared. Prisoners spent most of their time sitting or lying on their bunks. Especially, we hated being called out to be counted; and invariably we would be harangued and abused each time by the officer in charge of the roll-call. Pigs and dogs were the gentlest epithets he addressed us with while counting went on.

The atmosphere in the camp was tense and hostile, and we doubted our ability to survive to the end of the war. The bombing of Germany night and day and the inflammatory articles on the loss of life put us in the category of murderers. Americans recently shot down were being sent to our camp, and the tales they told of their experiences after being shot down were hair-raising.

One young blond American air-gunner had baled out with the rest of his crew. They were lynched by the enraged civilians, who beat all of them to death with implements they carried in their hands, with the exception of the air-gunner. He had been beaten until he was unconscious and they thought he too was dead.

When he regained consciousness he found himself in a cart under the pile of bodies of his crew. The Germans were busy digging a mass grave for them. He was in a quandary, for if he let them know he was alive, they would kill him at once. On the other hand he did not relish being buried alive. While he was debating what to do, bombs began to fall and the digging party scurried off to the shelters. The air-gunner crawled out of the cart and stumbled away. He was fortunate that the police caught him. For many nights we were awakened by his shrieking and crying as the nightmare haunted his sleep.

Our lives were complicated by the erratic behaviour of the Security Officer of the camp, the young officer who had given the signal for the beating up. We thought he was a madman, and we were afraid of him. He played little games with us, a kind of Russian roulette with our lives.

One of his favourite tricks as we wandered about the compound was to appear suddenly at the wire fence surrounding us, clawing his way up, shouting at the guards to shoot at us. The guards, as unnerved as we were by the hysterical urgency of his voice, began to fire, some into the air and some into the compound. At the first sound of his voice we ran for the nearest hut and dived inside. We lay on the floor, fear gripping at our stomachs, while the occasional bullet thudded into the woodwork, and above the sound of the shouting his frenzied voice screamed at the guards.

One day he marched into the compound accompanied by a number of guards carrying an iron plate. First they placed the plate in the middle of the compound; then, ordering the prisoners out of the huts they locked the doors and marched out again. The Security Officer reappeared outside the wire, and the familiar words of his, urging the guards to shoot, echoed around the camp. This time there was no place for us to hide. Bullets whistled over our heads as the guards in the watch-towers opened up with their guns at the iron target. We dug like moles into the sandy soil as bullets spat into the sand or ricocheted off the plate and whined across the open spaces.

During those winter months of 1944 and the beginning of 1945 we lived dangerously. By now the Russian armies were advancing fast on the Eastern Front and the allies were close to the Rhine. Once again we were told to be ready to leave. Marching orders were given for the next day, Tuesday, 6th February.

I sorted out my few pitiful belongings, choosing to wear a thick pair of socks and an old pair of French army boots. What few rations we had we shared out. Into my haversack I put my few personal belongings, checked my overcoat, and purloined some string to tie round my two thin blankets; then I settled down for a last good night's sleep.

The Americans set off first, and it was not until midday that we were given the order to march. I had collected the contents of two Red Cross food parcels and stacked them neatly into my haversack; my blankets were rolled up and over my shoulder. My boots I had laced loosely for I was sure my feet would swell from the marching. The haversack I would carry on my back and I tried it out to make sure it fitted snugly against my shoulder blades.

It seemed strangely quiet in the camp now the Americans had gone. It had already a dilapidated look about it, doors swinging open, the ground covered with litter, the watch-towers empty and abandoned. I was glad to be leaving it—for me it held only unpleasant memories.

11

The March

"Tuesday, 6th February, 1945: The first day set off from Stalag Luft 6, Grosse Tychau 1200 hrs. Arrived at Naffin 1900 hrs. Distance 20 kilometres." This was an entry I made in a small book that I carried in my pocket.

On the day that we marched out of the camp, a party of some two hundred prisoners, the countryside was covered in snow, bleak and inhospitable. Behind the column trundled wagons and horses carrying the guards' equipment. Ahead strode the officer in charge of the party, a small man with a loud voice.

The day was cold and the wind unpleasant. We marched with a swing, our morale boosted by the knowledge that the Russians were not far behind and that we were marching westwards. Our bodies soon warmed to the exercise, and there was an easy rhythm to our step so that the first few miles flew by.

We halted for ten minutes, resting at the side of the road, while the Germans inspected their maps. Satisfied that they were following the correct route, they ordered us back on the road, and off we set once more. In those few minutes my limbs stiffened up. My rucksack was not as comfortably settled on my back as before. As the miles passed by I felt the weight of my rucksack growing steadily heavier. The straps chafed at my shoulders and I found myself constantly adjusting them to ease the pressure. Ahead of me a prisoner undid his pack, took out tins of food, and threw them in the ditch. He was suffering from the same discomfort, and as a remedy was throwing away precious food. Others followed his example. For some distance the road was littered with tins of food and even articles of clothing.

The guards too began to feel the pace, and soon the wagons were laden with Germans resting their sore feet while we plodded on and on. Snow began to fall, and the day turned to night. It was then that everyone realized that the officer leading us had lost his way. We stood waiting on the road, cursing inwardly, while he looked at his map with the aid of a torch; then at a signal we struggled back the way we had come, until at last some miles back we came to a farm. Barn doors were opened and we rushed in, looking for a corner where there might be straw. Fully-dressed, my boots on my feet and my blankets wrapped round me, I fell asleep.

In the morning I found my feet had swollen in my boots. Feeling hungry, I took out a tin of stew. There was no way of heating it, but it tasted good just the same.

For the next few days we marched westwards through villages and towns: Zetlow, Roman, Pribbernow, Recknow, the names signposts in the memory. At midday we would halt by the roadside for a rest, foraging in our rucksacks for the food to keep us alive. Each night we would stop at a farm and bed down in a barn. If the resources of the farmer allowed it, we would be given two or three potatoes to eat, cooked by volunteers among the prisoners. A cup of hot mint tea followed, as well as a ration of food from our rucksacks.

Thursday, 15th February, was different. In the early hours of the morning we were lined up on the road and informed that we would be marching through a prohibited area that day. Anybody who fell out of the column would be shot.

Over the next ten hours we slogged our way across

country, driven on by the guards. When anybody weakened and fell behind, he was clubbed back into the column. Twice we were allowed a rest of a few minutes duration and then we were on our way again, heads lowered, nobody talking. The only thing that mattered was putting one foot in front of the other. It was no comfort to us to see guards taking turns at riding on the wagons, while the others, refreshed from their rest, drove us on and on.

As the day wore on and we began to weaken, our leader Vic Clark, summoning up his reserves of energy, moved up and down the column urging us on, boosting our morale and assisting others to keep the weaker ones going. Time and again his voice would ring out, encouraging, exhorting, cajoling, never allowing us to flag. At one stage when he drew up alongside and we chatted for a few minutes, I noticed how tired and grey he looked. The suggestion I made that he should ease up, was treated with scorn that belied the agony that showed on his face. He fell back to the rear of the column, to speed up those that were lagging.

The day wore on, as mile succeeded mile. My feet were swollen again and my legs had lost all feeling. Towards evening the temperature dropped well below freezing-point, the cold wind cut through my clothes and pinched my face. Day had turned into night, when the order was given for us to halt. We stood on the road, facing towards a common or small heath lit by a ring of small searchlights.

A voice over a hailer informed us that we would have to bed down on the ground for the night. A mobile kitchen had been set up, and we would be given hot soup later.

Covered in snow and ice, the heath was devoid of any tree or bush. I teamed up with Ray Chown and together we walked about the heath until the call came for us to collect our hot soup. We shuffled behind a long winding queue until it was our turn to be given a mug half-full of soup. It warmed my stomach, and revived me for a few minutes.

Together, Chown and I scoured the ground for a likely place to sleep. It made little difference where we rested, but we chose a hump that seemed to have less ice and snow than the rest. By agreement we placed two blankets on the ground, and lay down on them with our greatcoats tightly wrapped around our bodies. Using our rucksacks as pillows, we pulled the remaining two blankets over us to keep out the biting wind and snuggled hard against each other to keep ourselves warm.

Exhaustion overcame the awful physical forces that surrounded me, and I fell asleep; but not for long. I woke to find my body numb with cold, and my teeth chattering audibly. The blankets underneath me and my clothes were half sodden, half frozen. Climbing to my feet, I thumped at my body and stamped my feet. Chown staggered up beside me, and together we tramped up and down seeking to warm our limbs. I was so exhausted that my eyes kept closing, my body felt like an inert mass, heavy and shapeless.

Around us men staggered about like souls in torment, their arms flailing, their bodies casting weird shadows in the glare of the lights. Others sat on their haunches or lay stretched out on the ice. Many times that night, I crawled in between the blankets to die, and just as many times I crawled out of them again to beat myself back to life.

Morning came at last, but it brought little relief. We hauled our frozen bodies on to the road, and marched for nine hours, covering only twenty-four kilometres. Our route took us through Swinemunde and Pinchow, then on to Gonke. Over the next four days we covered sixty miles. Each day we marched, the distances covered grew shorter, although the time taken covered the whole day.

February turned into March, and still we kept on the move. Like the Israelites, we stayed a few days here, one or two days there, pitching our tents so to speak, and then moving on. Time and distance had no significance, the will to survive was everything. Our food had run out, and we relied on the Germans to supply us with enough to keep us alive. There was little forthcoming; occasionally a few potatoes, rarely a piece of bread. Our numbers dwindled. Where there had been 200 of us there now seemed less than half that number.

We got little sympathy or encouragement from the officer leading our column, frustrated and furious as he was with the thankless task of keeping us on the road. Almost every day he would harangue the guards in front of us, yelling that we were murderers who had killed and maimed innocent women and children, destroyed their homes, and showed no mercy when we dropped bombs on them. He urged them to treat us as such, giving no quarter, to shoot anyone they caught committing an act that seemed hostile to them. That man, by his speeches, gave us every incentive to keep marching.

Lack of food made us rash. Despite the warnings we searched for food and stole it where possible. One evening we were given raw vegetables to eat. Instinctively we gathered in small groups. I found an old bucket, collected some wood for a fire, somebody else found a water tap and soon we were huddled round the fire waiting for the vegetables to cook. Another member of the group, out searching for more firewood, returned with a bundle of sticks and sat down in the midst of us. Looking around to see that no guard was around he pulled a dead chicken from under his greatcoat. We began to pluck away at the feathers, when guards came round the corner. Whether or not they knew a chicken had been stolen was immaterial. Without hesitation, feathers and all, the chicken went into the pot, pushed down under the vegetables. They moved from group to group. We held our breath as they stopped to see what we were doing, praying that the chicken would not choose that moment to rise to the top. All was well, and the guards went on their way.

It was a disgusting meal of vegetables, chicken and feathers, and it lacked salt. We did our best to enjoy it, and it filled our stomachs, though I spent the night coughing up feathers.

As our plight became more and more desperate, we began to isolate ourselves from each other. It was as though we understood that nobody had any more strength left to help others. We closed in on ourselves, silent and dogged, conserving our energy, seeking only to survive each day. I began to count each step I took, drawing sustenance from the fact that each step brought me closer to home.

One night there was no food for the prisoners, and I searched around for something to eat. A locked door seemed a likely place, and with a long nail I widened a crack I found in the panelling. Grain dribbled out through the hole and, finding a tin, I half-filled it, poured water on the grain, stirred it and ate it. During the night my stomach began to swell and I rolled in agony all through the night.

Another time I tried to cook a sugar beet over a few burning sticks of wood, cutting off the soft top layer as it cooked and putting the beet back on the fire. Again I spent a sleepless night trying to combat the nauseating symptoms that affected my stomach. I was getting so hungry that when I saw some potato peelings trampled in the mud I scooped them up and ate them.

At one farm we were told that if anybody would volunteer to dig out potatoes from a clamp, wash them and cook them the prisoners could have food to eat. Only three or four of us volunteered. We dug away the

The March

earth and collected the potatoes, which we washed and put into a vat. Collecting wood for the fire, we soon had the water boiling merrily. The outhouse in which we boiled the potatoes contained another vat, which we filled with water and boiled to make mint tea. The prisoners queued up, and we served out the food and drink, then adjourned to the outhouse which was now warm and snug.

Leaning against the wall was an old tin bath. We filled it with hot water, and took it in turns to soak ourselves in it. Primitive though it was, and though the water was dirty by the time I took my turn, I enjoyed the luxury of it, my first bath for years.

The further westward we marched, the greater the risk we ran of being attacked by allied aircraft. Each day, far above us, planes flying in formation droned towards their targets in the heartland of Germany. There was a real danger that any low-flying aircraft might mistake us for an infantry unit on the march. Orders were given that we were to dive into the ditch nearest to us at the first sign of an attack.

During my time on the march there was only one such incident. An allied plane appeared low over the trees ahead of us. Above and behind followed another aircraft. We dived for the sides of the road, all except for a few foolhardy and excited prisoners who stood waving at the planes. Luckily for us the leading pilot had the sense to make sure of his target first. They swooped low over our heads, soaring up in a tight arc only to come roaring in again almost at ground level. Once again they rose skyward, then at five hundred feet they flew past waggling their wings. We jumped to our feet, waving and shouting with delight. Other formations of prisoners on the march were not so lucky, and many were killed by attacking allied aircraft, their pilots mistaking the prisoners for Germans.

Another day on the march; the rain pouring down

ceaselessly. Wet and hungry, we trudged on our way, until early in the afternoon we reached the farm which was our billet for the night. Miserably we bunked down in the barn. There was no food for us. Listless, we lay listening to the rain pounding on the roof. It was one of those rare moments when I wanted to give up the struggle. There was no future. Life was just one barn after another, only each time one felt weaker and less resolute, mind and body sickened by years of privations, humiliation and degradation.

One of the lads, peering out of the barn door, suddenly beckoned us to join him. Outside in the pelting rain, women dressed in sacking were appearing, carrying buckets of hot soup. They stopped some distance from the barn and stood silent and still, waiting. Each one of them had such dignity, though the rain lashed their faces and bodies. Astonishingly, nobody rushed, as was their wont, to queue up for the food. Instead they walked, quietly waiting while the women doled out the food until none was left.

They were Polish women, used as slave labour, who lived in hovels on the farm, the open window spaces covered with sacking to keep out the rain. Recognizing us as prisoners of war, they had collected the meagre resources that they had saved, mainly beans, and cooked them over their fires and come out into the rain to feed us. Those women gave us back our dignity and our strength, as well as giving us food. There seemed no adequate way in which to express our thanks.

Suddenly, for the moment, the marching was over. We were put into wagons and transported overnight to Fallingbostel. There we stayed for nearly two weeks, living under canvas with little or no food to eat. I sold my watch for two loaves of bread. I considered it a good bargain.

12

The Final Escape

Germany was falling apart. The Allies were crossing the Rhine, while the Russians were sweeping towards Berlin. Mighty armies fighting without mercy; while above, the sky was black with planes loaded with destruction. In the eye of the storm were these small groups of prisoners and refugees struggling westward, the flotsam and jetsam, the debris of war; frightened men and women and children, hostages of the fortunes of one side or the other. Everybody was waiting. It was as though a huge tidal wave could be seen at a distance moving inexorably towards us, reaching ever nearer to engulf us and destroy. Meanwhile we floated gently to and fro in waters deceptively calm, each one of us a human being, planning in his tiny mind how he could survive the holocaust yet to come. But for all our planning, could any of us expect to survive? So as the holocaust drew nearer we waited, helpless and afraid.

It was now the end of March 1945. Some official reached a decision. We were to march again, and rumour stated that our destination was to be Lübeck on the Baltic coast. This meant that we would be retracing our footsteps again, marching back to the East. As soon as we set off the next morning the rumours were partly confirmed, for we were marching eastwards. Many of the prisoners were now too weak to march, and were left behind. The rest of us, a hotchpotch of men, mainly American and English aircrew, trudged out of the camp and onto the road.

My mind rejected completely the idea of turning my back on the road to home. At the first opportunity I would leave the column and continue westwards on my own. The risks were enormous, and I knew that no mercy would be shown to me if I was caught. Yet were my chances any better by staying with the column?

We moved at a slow pace, for there was not much strength left in any of us. It was not long before the first order was given to fall out by the roadside for a few minutes' rest. I had already slipped back down the column, waiting for an opportune moment to take my leave. At this moment, an army P.O.W., who introduced himself as MacDonald, perched himself on the bank beside me. He asked me what I was up to. He had watched me dropping back, and had already half-guessed my intentions. If I was going to escape, could he join forces with me? I liked him. He had a durable quality to him and a sense of humour. Although I had always worked on my own, I felt happy at the thought of his company, and I agreed.

Back on the road once more, the two of us straggled along at the back of the column, allowing a gap to open up between us and the main column. It was then that we were joined by an American called Strafford. We told him that it would be better for him to rejoin the main group, as we were going to make a run for it. He said it was fine with him, but if we were going to make a break, he was going with us. His determination was strong enough for us to agree without too much discussion.

The gap between us and the column soon widened appreciably, and only one obstacle lay between us and escape. Two guards had fallen back with us, and marched a few steps to our rear. By now I had stiffened one leg to give the appearance of a limp, an action followed by my two comrades. In any other circumstances it would have been quite a comical sight. It had little effect on the guards. They were nervous and worried, and shouted at us to catch up with the others. We did so for a few paces, then slowed up again. They grew angry as the column ahead disappeared round a bend in the road, and threatened to shoot us if we did not catch up immediately. Another guard on a bicycle came into view from the direction of the column, and slithered to a stop beside our guards. The three of them stood in the middle of the road, arguing angrily with each other and gesticulating towards us. The signs did not augur well for us, so we forgot our limps and put on speed as unobtrusively as we could.

On reaching the bend in the road, we looked back, to see the guards, now some distance behind us, still remonstrating with each other. The column was some 200 yards ahead. Now was the moment. We dashed off the road and into the trees close by, running madly to put as much distance as we could between the guards and ourselves.

We stopped running and crouched down in the undergrowth, listening for any sound of pursuit. All we could hear was our own heavy breathing as our lungs worked overtime. After a short rest, we moved on through the countryside in a westerly direction, taking advantage of any cover that trees or hedges could give us, making our way carefully across fields and meadows. By now it was late afternoon, and we would soon need a safe place to hide. Ahead of us lay a small copse, and beyond it some farm buildings. We were on a ridge, and below us in the valley we could see a road winding its way between farm buildings and isolated cottages.

We crept towards the farm ahead of us, our eager eyes and ears alert to any danger that might threaten. There were no signs of life. We threaded our way between barns and outhouses, crouching at the corner of the buildings and peering round them, then moving

The Lonely Path To Freedom

on to another vantage point. What we needed now was food and water, and a place to hide.

We slipped through an open door into a large kitchen. Two women, one young, one old, sprang to their feet with cries of alarm. I spoke to them in broken German, and found out that their menfolk were away fighting and that they were having to keep the farm going on their own. Promising them that no harm would come to them, I asked them to provide us with food and drink. Evidently relieved, they moved purposefully around the kitchen, and soon we were sitting down to a meal of boiled eggs and bread, followed by coffee.

The food was wholesome and pleasant, but our own position was unreal. We sat in the kitchen eating and drinking; the women, scared and silent, cut bread for us and refilled our cups. Outside the kitchen a dreadful war was being fought. There was no reason why at any moment German soldiers should not enter the kitchen and mow us down. Yet still we lingered, our stomachs full, savouring the warmth of the coffee, each one of us unable to make the next decision. The old woman left the kitchen but no one moved to follow her.

She returned visibly agitated, and pleaded with us to go. German soldiers would be coming soon and it would put her life in danger as well as ours. Her alarm was real, and I knew it was time for us to leave.

There was a sound of low-flying aircraft and the rattle of machine-guns and cannon firing. We ran out into the courtyard to see allied aircraft zooming above the valley in the direction from which we had come, firing as they flew. They wheeled up into the air then went flying in, firing again and again. My stomach turned over as I estimated that the column of prisoners I had so recently left could not be far from the position the planes were attacking. My fears were justified: I found out later that the column had just arrived at a farm to bed down for the night, when the planes arrived, and on seeing the

The Final Escape

German guards below immediately went into the attack. Many prisoners were killed, including a number I had known so well for so many years. It was a tragedy that was repeated in other places.

We stole across the courtyard and round the outlying buildings, when suddenly we were confronted by two strange-looking dirty creatures, who identified themselves as Russians. They were being used as slave labour on the farm. Like us they knew a little German. We said that we were prisoners of war, and were on the run. Telling us that they would look after us if we would trust them, they led us into a wood close by. In a hollow among the trees, they uncovered a small chamber dug out of the earth. I surmised that it was either a small crude air-raid shelter or a hideway for themselves when things became dangerous.

They told us that German soldiers were in the vicinity, and that it would be safer to hide in the dug-out till nightfall. When the coast was clear they would take us back to the farm and find a hiding-place for us in one of the barns. We had little choice but to trust them, so we clambered down into the hole. An improvised trapdoor blotted out the light, and we could hear them muttering to each other as they dragged branches over the door to camouflage the entrance. We crouched, huddled together in the dark damp hole, and waited.

Hours later the trapdoor was opened, and our Russian friends beckoned us to climb out and follow them. The night was black and still. We followed them back to the farm we had left earlier. Opening one of the barn doors, the Russians slipped inside and we followed. They guided us up a ladder into a loft above, made sure that we were bedded down for the night, promised that they would return the next day with food, and left us to ourselves.

I lay in the straw, snug and warm, but I could not sleep. My mind was a mass of doubts. The war was nearly over. I had needed only to stay with the column and eventually I would have been released and sent home with the others. But I had committed myself to escaping, and there was no turning back. Either I would succeed, or I would die. I was certain that the Germans, fanatically defending what was left of their country, would not waste time taking prisoners. For nearly four years I had survived precariously; now with the war nearly over I had put myself in a position where my first mistake would be my last. I fell into an uneasy sleep.

The Russians crouching at my feet woke me. It was morning, and they had come with an offering of potatoes and milk. The potatoes had been cooked for the pigs, but they had put some aside for us. Their information was that the Allies had crossed the Rhine in force, and were moving fast across Germany. We could stay hidden in the barn until the Allies arrived. It would not be long, and in the meantime they would keep us supplied with food as often as they could. But they warned us that Germans were around everywhere; we must be careful, under no circumstances were we to go outside the barn.

After eating the potatoes, we reconnoitred our hideout. It was a large barn with a concrete floor. At one end, two large hinged doors formed the entrance. Large farm implements such as ploughs and rakes were drawn up side by side, placed in the barn to keep them in good condition while the men were away. Hand tools hung on the wall.

At the opposite end to the entrance a ladder was lashed to the side of the barn. It led up to the loft in which we were hiding, reaching up through an open trapdoor. The loft floor was made up of large planks which rested on the cross beams and covered three-quarters of the barn. The area left uncovered was above the barn doors, so that if one stood at the end of the planking one could look down into the barn below. The remainder of the loft floor was a skeleton of beams crisscrossing each other, except for one corner which had half-a-dozen planks, cut to size, fitting snugly where the roof met the wall. These planks held a small amount of loose straw. The main loft floor was covered with bales of straw and more loose straw.

Half-way along from the open trapdoor we arranged the straw to make a nest for ourselves. Above us the roof was covered with wooden slats, except for a fanlight which could be reached with difficulty if one straddled the beams that supported the roof.

For the next three days we waited for something to happen. Each day the Russians would visit us for a few minutes, bringing us potatoes and milk. Each day they told us that the Allies were getting nearer and would soon be here. The hours dragged by interminably, but we were afraid to move from the confines of the loft.

The fourth day dawned, and we listened as we had for the past three days, for the distant sounds of gunfire that would bring us hope that soon we would be free men. We heard nothing. Morning turned to afternoon, and we lay quietly in our nest talking softly to each other.

Below us the barn door creaked. Somebody was down there. The door creaked again, and there came a rustling sound as though a horde of rats had invaded the place. This sound spread throughout the barn, and we cowered down, looking at each other in silent astonishment. With sudden violence the barn door crunched open, followed by the roar of a German-speaking voice, and the sounds of blows and howls of pain. From the yelling below, we realized that a number of Russian prisoners had entered the barn in search of food. The guard had discovered them, and was beating them out of the barn with his rifle. Then, silence; the Russians had gone, but we sensed that the guard was below, listening. Suspended in our fear, we waited. He moved. We could hear his footsteps on the ladder, rung by rung. I cursed the Russians for picking the barn we were hiding in to look for food.

Crouched in the nest, I peered through the straw. The guard's head and shoulders appeared above the trapdoor. He stood there, head at half-cock as he gazed down the length of the barn, listening for the sound of any movement. Motionless for a full minute he stood, while we held our breath; then he moved back down the ladder. The barn door creaked, and all was still; but yet we would not stir, until uncertainty became certainty, and we moved cautiously out of our hiding-place to look over the barn. He was gone, and the crisis was over.

I knew though, that if there was any repetition of such an incident, we might not be so lucky. We had to find a new hiding-place in the barn. The obvious place was the isolated corner of the loft, with its half-a-dozen planks and its cover of loose straw. To reach it we would have to straddle a narrow beam for some ten feet, with a drop of some twelve to fourteen feet to the concrete below if one slipped; nevertheless it was a safer place than the one we were in.

Gathering together our belongings we dragged them along the beam. We also brought over more straw, enough to cover the three of us if another marauding party should enter the barn. The sloping roof above our heads made it impossible for us to stand, and there was just sufficient room for us to lie down curled up.

The rest of the day passed uneventfully. We were bored and frustrated by the confines of the barn, and unsettled by the incident earlier in the day. We spent our time telling stories and giving each other an account of our life-history. MacDonald told us that his profession during peacetime was that of a burglar. I did not know whether to believe him or not. He had a sense of humour, and a poker-faced delivery that gave nothing away. I was glad of his company. The stories he regaled us with were fascinating and improbable.

Just before dark our Russian allies arrived with potatoes. They were anxious and excited, telling us that the Germans were retreating fast, and that the front line of the battle was not far away. We were warned that a German fighting unit would be arriving the next day, and that we were to remain hidden. With that information they disappeared. So many emotions coursed through my veins I could not sleep that night. Neither could the others, and we whispered to each other until far into the night.

All through the next day we lay holed-up in the corner of the loft, listening for any sound that might confirm what the Russians had told us. It was close to nightfall when we heard the grinding of tank tracks on the road leading up to the farm. The roar of revving engines vibrated through the barn, as we lay tensely awaiting the visitors, unwelcome ones. As they ground in and around the farm buildings, one after the other, the intensity of noise was shattering. Then came the hoarse shouting of men giving orders, and the sound of countless feet running here and there.

I shivered where I lay, fighting the thought that we had trapped ourselves. Why had we not thought of transferring to the dug-out in the woods when we knew the Germans were coming? Not that it made any difference now, it was too late. We were surrounded by the enemy. With so much traffic around the farm surely they must use the barns for sleeping quarters! With a sinking feeling in my stomach, I listened for the barn doors to open.

The shouting went on, the sounds of metal striking on metal and the occasional revving up of an engine rent the air, but still the barn doors remained shut. Darkness had fallen for some time, yet we had not moved a muscle nor do I think we even breathed.

The noises died away, and for a while all was silent.

We relaxed a little, and moved our limbs gently to restore the circulation. Soon we began to whisper to each other, only to be cut short by the sound of a cough outside the barn, just below us. Whoever it was began to stamp his feet, then moved a few steps one way, then another, but always returning to the spot just below us. It did not take us long to understand that the Germans had posted a soldier on sentry-duty, next to the spot where we were hiding. All would be well, as long as none of us made a sound, for in the still night air the occasional cough of the sentry exploded in our ears.

I must have fallen asleep, for I awoke to find somebody coughing loudly. It was myself. My two companions were thumping me to wake up, and one had his hand over my mouth in a vain attempt to silence me. Blind panic seized me for a moment, and I drew in great gulps of air; then I lay still, my blood curdling with fear. A voice rang out, loudly demanding who was there. A short silence then the question was repeated. The next moment a whistle blew shrill and loud. It blasted again and again. Within seconds came the sound of running feet, of shouting men, then the voice of the sentry explaining his actions. There was bedlam again, more orders, then the sound of rifle bolts being drawn.

The barn doors swung open, and down below, as I peered through a space between the planks, a line of soldiers spread across the barn, torches shining in their hands. Step by step they searched the floor below. Then once again came that dreadful sound of feet on the rungs of the ladder. Turning my head slightly, I could see the dim shapes of the soldiers in the light of their torches, as they climbed into the loft and spread out once again across the barn. I could see, too, the glint of the rifles and of the bayonets fixed to them, as they prodded into the straw.

Step by step, with monstrous certainty, they worked their way towards us, stopping only when they reached the end of the planking. Then, as one man they blazed their torches onto the heap of straw under which we were hiding. The light dazzled my eyes and I closed them tightly. All this time, terrified, I prayed to God as I had never prayed before. And all the while they stood in a line, their torches flashing to and fro over us, muttering to each other, motionless except for the movement of the lights. Our lives ticked away second by second, and still there was no movement.

Abruptly the line of soldiers broke up. They were leaving. One by one they descended the ladder. The barn door closed, and all was still, except once more the sound of stamping feet below us, as the sentry worked to keep them warm. The night dragged on and on, as we lay there, still, like effigies in a church.

Daylight filtered through the fanlight in the roof. With it came a spate of activity outside. Once more the blowing of whistles and shouting of orders. Above all this surge of sound came the sudden explosive roar of a gun being fired. More guns opened up and a crescendo of noise ripped again and again through the barn. I clapped my hands to my ears but it made little difference.

The guns stopped as suddenly as they started. Engines roared into life, and within minutes the enemy had gone, leaving only the faint sound of their trucks on the road as they moved away from the farm. They had gone, and we were still alive.

For hours we waited there, lying tense and silent, not daring to venture from our hiding-place. It was MacDonald who first heard the faint sounds of firing in the distance. Bidding us to stay where we were, he crept away over the beams and disappeared among the bales at the far end. We waited. Suddenly his voice reached us, urgent and excited. Scrambling out of our hiding-place, we found him near the trapdoor, a young German soldier on his knees beside him.

MacDonald informed us grimly that this was an SS

trooper, and that he had come upon him lying in the straw. It had been stalemate, the two crouching and watching each other warily, until MacDonald called us up as reinforcements. He was sure the German had arms hidden in the straw, and made him move over to the centre of the barn and lie down. Where there was one man there might be others, within the vicinity of the barn; we would have to keep quiet and stay still.

While we watched our prisoner, MacDonald climbed up to the fanlight in the roof and looked out. After a few moments he came down, telling me to have a look for myself. I scrambled up and poked my head up level with the fanlight.

Through the window I could see out over the valley. On the far side a number of tanks manoeuvred round some farm buildings. As I watched, long arcs of fire exploded from a flame-thrower on one of them, savaging the buildings and setting them on fire. The rattle of machine guns, and the dull sound of exploding shells filled the air.

The sight of flame-throwers at work sickened me. There had to be Germans inside the buildings, making a stand. If MacDonald was right, and there were Germans around the barn, what chance would we have, trapped between the two sides? As if in answer to my thought, I heard the sound of a tank moving up the road towards the barn. I slid down the beams and rejoined the others. We could hear the engine roaring and revving while the metal tracks screeched their way towards us. For an eternity we sat, frozen in fearful anticipation, as the tank moved nearer, stopped and moved again, as though spying out the land for any hidden dangers.

From the corner of the barn we heard the crack of a rifle, from another spot came a second shot. The Germans were sniping at the tank. As our minds registered the sounds the tank opened up with its machine-guns, spraying the barn with bullets. They came flying through the slatted wooden walls, pinging and ricocheting off the machinery below. Blindly and instinctively, I jumped down onto the concrete floor below and scrambled under one of the mechanical farm pieces. Curling up into a ball with my arms wrapped round my head, I lay like an unborn babe, while the battle raged around me. My two companions did not question my movements, but followed me down, and like me were curled up under pieces of farming equipment.

The tank screeched and screamed, moving here and there, firing furiously in long bursts. Rifles cracked around us. Bullets seemed to fill the air, and their impact on the machinery under which we were hidden added a strange musical note to the cacophony of sounds that filled the barn. I was grateful that the Allies were short of flame-throwers for the occasion.

Suddenly the rifle-fire ceased. The tank careered back and forth firing bursts into the barn, then it too stopping firing. There was silence for a few moments, except for the revving of the engine, then came the sound of the tank returning down the road. I crept out from my hiding-place, followed by the others, and softly climbed the ladder back up to the loft. Our prisoner had disappeared, but I was not unhappy. The possibility of being gunned down by him while our backs were turned had been ever-present in my mind.

We held a council of war, and decided that the most sensible thing to do was to remain where we were. There was no point in going out to meet trouble. We had had enough of it already, and miraculously we had survived. The barn was a safe place. Besides, with Germans all around us we had more than enough company.

Time crawled by as we lay in the straw, waiting. The firing was spasmodic and venomous, but insulated as we were within the barn it seemed remote and indifferent. The events of the past twenty-four hours had dried up all my emotions, and unless I was on the receiving end of any action, I could no longer react to the sounds of battle.

With a crash the barn doors flew open. As we rose from the straw, startled, ready for action, the two faces of our Russian friends appeared above the trapdoor. They shouted that the tanks were everywhere, and that we must come and see for ourselves. Their excitement was too much for us, and like kids we scrambled down the ladder, half-falling to the ground. As we rushed into the courtyard the Russians signalled to us to get down. We crouched close to the ground and looked around.

In the middle of the courtyard a German soldier lay on his back moaning, his leg smashed by bullets. Around the edge of the farm buildings, people were lying spread-eagled on the ground peering into the valley. They were the slave labour force, all waiting for the moment of release. An old man lay by a ditch, a while tablecloth on the ground beside him. Everywhere within the precincts of the farm men lay motionless, waiting.

I looked out across the valley. Line upon line of tanks moved slowly across the land. It was such a mighty force of armour it took my breath away. Dotted about the valley were burning buildings, flames flickering in the morning air. The firing had stopped but the tanks in line astern moved purposefully onwards.

This was the moment I had waited for for so long. All those terrible years in captivity passed through my mind and fell away. The moment I had dreamed of had come, and I could wait no longer.

Crouching, I ran across the courtyard, and kneeling down beside the old man, snatched up the tablecloth. He yelled at me to get down, the tanks were firing at anything that moved, and that I would be killed.

Heedless of his advice I rose to my feet, the cloth

already whirling above my head, and ran out into the field that sloped down into the valley; and as I ran, I yelled and shouted that I had been a prisoner of war and now I was free. On either side of me, some distance behind, MacDonald and Strafford were following, shouting and waving their arms. They were not going to be left behind.

The turrets of the tanks swung slowly round until their guns pointed towards us. I began to curse and rant, all the pent-up feelings and emotions of the past four years giving emphasis to my frantic need to be recognized.

In the middle of the line, a tank stopped. One after another they ground to a halt. A hatch opened and a head appeared, angled and alert to the sound of voices. Suddenly figures climbed out of the hatches and jumped to the ground. One huge figure of a man stood in front of his tank, watching and listening. I shouted louder, my voice hoarse, slandering him in good basic English. He understood, for he started walking towards me, then breaking into a run, a huge grin spreading over his face. Men from the other tanks followed him. I ran stumbling and cursing and crying into his arms.

With one movement he swept me off the ground and swung me round and round, a wonderful grin on his face, while the tears coursed down his cheeks.

This mountain of a man who swept me up in his arms introduced himself as 'Tiny' Bennett from Hackney Road in London. We were the first English prisoners they had met. It was a great moment for them.

We were submerged by a mob of cheering tank men, and as they half-carried us with them those still in the tanks stood up and cheered and cheered, their voices echoing up and down the valley.

It was the 15th April 1945, and I was a free man.